Room at the Inn/Minnesota

Guide to Minnesota's Historic B&Bs,
Hotels and Country Inns

Laura Zahn

Down to Earth Publications
St. Paul, Minnesota

Published by **Down to Earth Publications**
1426 Sheldon
St. Paul, MN 55108

Distributed by **Voyageur Press**
123 Second St.
Stillwater, MN 55082
1-800-888-WOLF or **612-430-2210**

First printing, November 1988

Library of Congress Cataloging in Publication Data.
Zahn, Laura Claire
    Room at the Inn/Minnesota
    Guide to Minnesota's Historic B&Bs, Hotels and Country Inns

1. Bed and Breakfast Accommodations - Middle West - Directories
TX 907.

ISBN 0-939301-04-0 (softcover)

Map by Jim Miller

Photos by Laura Zahn, except the photo of Young's Island B&B, which was taken by Jim Miller

Pictured on the cover (and art provided by):
    Upper Left Corner - Mrs. B's Historic Lanesboro Inn, Lanesboro
    Upper Right Corner - Red Gables Inn, Lake City
    Lower Left Corner - The Archer House, Northfield
    Lower Right Corner - Canterbury Inn B&B, Rochester

Printing by BookCrafters, Ann Arbor, Michigan

To Jim,

with whom I would like to stay

in these places,

again and again...

Special thanks to Kristina Ford, Mary and Ed Zahn, Leslie Dimond, Jim Miller, and old and new friends in special places. Thanks, too, to the innkeepers who re-arranged their schedules or otherwise went out of their ways to assist me.

Table of Contents

Please Note: Driving times from the Twin Cities Metro Area may vary depending on starting point, speed and road conditions.

-Within 2 hours of the Twin Cities

-Within 3 hours of the Twin Cities

-Worth the Drive

Extras

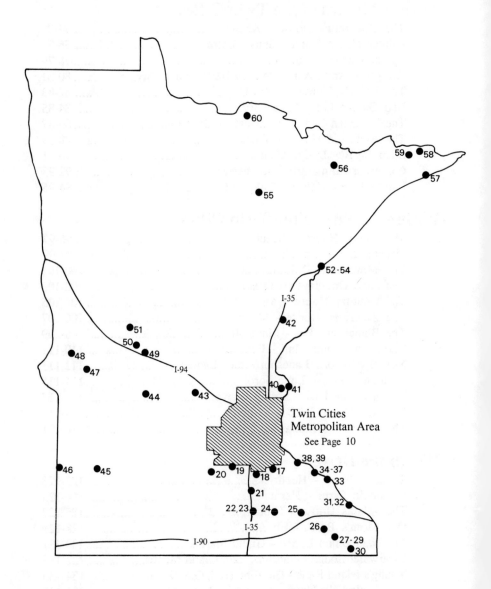

Twin Cities
Metropolitan Area
See Page 10

#1-16 - See Twin Cities Area Map, next page
17. Quill & Quilt - Cannon Falls
18. The Archer House - Northfield
19. Schumacher's New Prague Hotel - New Prague
20. The Cosgrove - LeSueur
21. The Hutchinson House - Faribault
22. Northrop House - Owatonna
23. The Tudor on Bridge - Owatonna
24. Eden B&B - Dodge Center
25. Canterbury Inn B&B - Rochester
26. Lund's Guest House - Chatfield
27. Carrolton Country Inn - Lanesboro
28. Mrs. B's Historic Lanesboro Inn - Lanesboro
29. Scanlan House - Lanesboro
30. Touch of the Past - Spring Grove
31. Carriage House B&B - Winona
32. The Hotel - Winona
33. The Anderson House - Wabasha
34. Evergreen Knoll Acres Country B&B - Lake City
35. The Rahilly House - Lake City
36. Red Gables Inn - Lake City
37. The Victorian Bed & Breakfast - Lake City
38. The Pratt-Taber Inn - Red Wing
39. The St. James Hotel - Red Wing
40. Country Bed and Breakfast - Shafer
41. Historic Taylors Falls Jail - Taylors Falls
42. The Governor's House - Askov
43. Thayer Hotel - Annandale
44. Spicer Castle - Spicer
45. The Blanchford Inn - Marshall
46. Triple L Farm - Hendricks
47. The American House - Morris
48. Lawndale Farm - Herman
49. Palmer House Hotel - Sauk Centre
50. Just Like Grandma's - Osakis
51. The Country House - Miltona
52. The Ellery House - Duluth
53. Fitger's Inn - Duluth
54. The Mansion - Duluth
55. The Adams House - Hibbing
56. Our Mom's B&B - Ely
57. The Naniboujou Lodge - Grand Marais
58. Clearwater Lodge - Gunflint Trail, Grand Marais
59. Young's Island B&B - Gunflint Trail, Grand Marais
60. The Kettle Falls Hotel - Voyageurs National Park

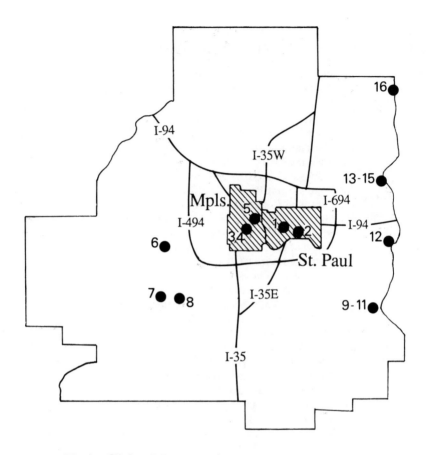

Twin Cities Metropolitan Area

1. Chatsworth B&B - St. Paul
2. Yoerg House - St. Paul
3. Evelo's B&B - Minneapolis
4. Linné Bed & Breakfast - Minneapolis
5. Nicollet Island Inn - Minneapolis
6. Christopher Inn - Excelsior
7. Bluff Creek Inn - Chaska
8. Sunny Morning Manor - Shakopee
9. Hazelwood - Hastings
10. The River Rose - Hastings
11. Thorwood B&B Inn - Hastings
12. The Afton House Inn - Afton
13. Lowell Inn - Stillwater
14. Overlook Inn - Stillwater
15. Rivertown Inn - Stillwater
16. Asa Parker House - Marine on the St. Croix

Introduction

What to Know about Using this Guide

For a very long time, it seemed that "getting away from it all" meant a week in the summer at the family cabin or at a resort housekeeping cottage.

But we have changed. Fewer people are waiting until retirement to enjoy traveling. More parents feel less guilty for making arrangements to leave the kids at home and getting away *from* them, instead of *with* them. Many two-career couples are so busy they rarely see each other.

We want to get away more often, for shorter periods of time, and stay closer to home. Three-day weekends now make up most of our "vacations."

And we want to treat ourselves. We don't seem to want super-slick city hotels or the stimulation of blaring TVs or ringing phones on these getaways. Instead, we're looking toward lodging in facilities that are warm and personal - right down to the decorating, the homey feeling often inspired by Early American decor and Victorian antiques. We want to return to a slower pace, if only for overnight. And we may want to rekindle some romance in a four-poster bed or a double whirlpool.

This book is intended as a guide to those getaways.

Why is this guide necessary?

This much credible information isn't available in any other single publication or in any consistent manner. Many of these establishments are very new and haven't been "written up" in articles or other guides. And most have limited advertising or public relations budgets, so they depend on word-of-mouth or an occasional feature story in a local paper to get out the word.

Also, many travelers don't know what B&Bs or country inns are, and many municipalities are giving prospective innkeepers a tremendously hard time because of ignorance. Perhaps this book will serve as an educational tool to spread the good news -- this is a *great* way to travel and a tourism asset in every community.

So, then, what is a B&B?

B&B stands for Bed and Breakfast. For years, travelers to Europe have enjoyed inexpensive accommodations in the extra bedroom of a local family's home. They found that B&Bs not only saved money and provided lodging in out-of-the-way places, but were a great way to meet friendly local people.

To say the B&B movement is catching on in America is a whopper of an understatement. The East and West coasts are loaded with them, and at least two glossy national magazines are devoted to B&Bs and country inns. In Minnesota, historic B&Bs are not necessarily economical, but they definitely remain a good way to meet neighbors. And they are much different than a motel or hotel.

At this writing, Minnesota does not have a legal definition of a B&B (but licensing of the facility is required through the Minnesota Department of Health).

A rough definition might be: A home, lived in by the owner or manager, which has one or more guest rooms for rent overnight, often sharing bathrooms and other common rooms, such as living and dining rooms, and which has some kind of breakfast available before check-out the next day included in the overnight rate.

From there, it's impossible to draw a picture of a typical B&B -- afterall, each place is different, and that is what is so appealing about them. Keep in mind that there is a wide variety of B&Bs in Minnesota: restored mansions, perhaps with elegant rooms offering whirlpool baths and fireplaces, designed for romantic weekend getaways; more modest restored homes; older homes that are not fancy at all and offer a lower-priced, more-European B&B experience for travelers; farm stays; northwoods retreats.

In general, most B&Bs are cozy and homey. It's common for guests to find themselves talking with other guests and the hosts in the living room at night, making arrangements to have dinner together, and sharing travel tips as they pass the breakfast platter the next morning.

Don't be afraid to try a B&B during your next trip or getaway. And, if the first one wasn't quite what you had envisioned, do try another -- they are all very different. To avoid disappointment, know your tastes and expectations and then find out what the place offers. This book is designed to help you find lodging that suits you.

What is a country inn?

A country inn doesn't have to be in the country. What makes it "country" is more its atmosphere and size. It's larger than a B&B -- roughly eight rooms or more -- but smaller than a hotel, and may be built in a large home or former small hotel. A country inn has some of the personal atmosphere of a B&B with some of the privacy of a hotel. Some amenities, like phones or TVs in the room, are more likely than in B&Bs. Breakfast may or may not be included in the room rate. Also, rooms usually are in the same structure (most often upstairs) as the kitchen, lobby and dining areas. Inns may be more likely to serve meals other than breakfast. Innkeepers are often willing and able to put on splendid weddings or other private parties (so will some B&B owners, so ask!).

Both at B&Bs and country inns, expect no bellhops, no elevator and no room service.

Suggestions for being a good guest

Most people who choose to travel this way are wonderful folks: quiet, easy-going and honest. It's rare, innkeepers say, to have a check bounce or find a towel missing. If you've never traveled this way, it might be helpful to point out a few hints that will ingratiate you with innkeepers.

The point, of course, is to feel at home. But remember it is someone else's home, and you are a guest. Don't call for reservations at midnight. Don't tie up their phone. Be thoughtful of other guests, especially if you smoke or are sharing bathrooms. Hosts will often provide information on local activities, but they are not tour guides. Remember, if you don't show up for your room and the innkeeper can't re-rent it (quite likely, since few B&Bs take "walk ins" and instead depend on advance reservations), he or she may be losing a half or a quarter of that night's income. So do keep in touch if plans change. If you honestly think you are a good guest when you visit friends or relatives, you will be a good B&B/inn traveler.

Who was selected to be included in this book?

First of all, only historic structures were included. "Historic" is roughly defined as 50 years or older and, hopefully, of some local historic significance. Several of the structures included in this guide are listed on the National Register of Historic Places, and all of them have interesting pasts.

Secondly, innkeepers were told their place needed to "feel" historic both inside and out. The history could be carried inside through Early American, Victorian or "country" decor or use of antiques. Therefore, historic homes or buildings which have been completely modernized and then turned into B&Bs were not included.

Unlike many guides, which make money both from readers buying the book and from innkeepers paying to be included, no one paid to be in this book. This book is intended to provide credible information for the benefit of readers/travelers, not as an advertising vehicle for innkeepers. Not all historic B&Bs or inns were selected for inclusion (see below).

Each facility which was included was personally visited by the author. Please do not think this counts as any kind of "inspection," as cleanliness and any other aspect of service may vary. Cleanliness or other concerns about the way business is conducted should be reported to health, business and tourism officials.

This book was intended as a guide to provide information, not an end-all-and-be-all rating service. In most cases, if facilities met the above criteria, they were included. The writing was intended to satisfy readers' interests on the historic nature of the home, who the innkeepers are, and why and how they got into innkeeping. It also was designed simply to describe the facilities of the B&B or inn, without many adjectives. Then readers can make their own choices according to their own tastes and preferences.

Note that in this edition, a list of contemporary B&Bs is included in the back. They have not been visited by the author; information was provided by innkeepers or the Minnesota Office of Tourism.

Who is not included?

Very few historic B&Bs or inns known to the author were left out. The reasons varied. A few historic structures were left out because they did not fit the above criteria, they did not seem to be the type of place which the audience of this book would want to visit, for various reasons, or because information could not be obtained, a visit could not be arranged, or innkeepers did not want the publicity at this time. Doubtless, some were left out because the author was not aware of them. Large hotels, resorts and wilderness lodges were not included, though there are many fine facilities available.

Part of the fun of traveling this way is getting to know the hosts. Therefore, B&Bs which are not independent (that is, they accept reservations only through a reservation service) have not been included. Arrangements can be made directly with each of the innkeepers listed in this guide.

Should you choose to use a reservation service, however, you may wish to contact Karen Anderson at Special Places, Inc., 4624 Highland Road, Minnetonka, MN 55345; 612-938-3326. Karen visits all B&Bs and inns she represents and is well-respected in the industry.

What readers should know about...

...**Rooms:** The number of rooms and some examples of decor and bathroom arrangements are explained. The space in this section was very limited, so please ask innkeepers for more complete information.

...**Rates:** Rates are current for all of 1988 and well into 1989, in most cases. If in doubt, assume about 5 percent increase per year. All rates are subject to change, however, and please do not call innkeepers nasty names if their rates have gone up.

Because rates often have little in common with what guests will get at hotels or motels for the same rate, here's a very general breakdown on what guests might get for their money:

$65 and up - Privacy is sometimes what you're buying here, since many of the inns in this price range are designed as romantic or cozy weekend getaways. The inns themselves have probably had major renovation and expert decoration, perhaps with designer linens or handmade quilts, for example. For this amount, something special usually is included, such as a bottle of wine and candies on the pillow at night, a private bath, air conditioning, and perhaps a whirlpool, working fireplace or lake view.

$40-$60 - These mid-priced lodgings may be worth every bit as much as the higher priced, except for one thing. Perhaps they do not offer fireplaces or whirlpools. Maybe they are located slightly out of town or in a town which won't support higher rates, or they have shared baths. Generally, you can expect tasteful decor and comfortable furnishings. And these are places that are smaller and where opportunities are greater to sit on the porch swing and talk with other guests or the owners, or have them sit down at the breakfast table with you.

$35 and Under - If you get what you pay for, why are they charging less? Often it's because relatively little money has been put into converting the home into a B&B. That means shared baths, perhaps rugs instead of carpeting, painted walls instead of wallpapered, occasionally modern ceilings, and the living room has dad's easy chair instead of chintz-covered designer furniture. Sometimes this price range simply means that a particular room is small, or the B&B is in an out-of-the-way spot that doesn't draw big tourism dollars. The low price doesn't mean the place isn't clean or otherwise perfectly OK.

...Tax: In addition to Minnesota sales tax of 6 percent, many municipalities levy a "bed tax" or "room tax," which overnight lodging facilities must charge. Commonly, that money is used to promote the community. Don't be surprised to have up to 10 percent total tax added to your bill.

...Shared baths:

Can we talk? Let's be frank. Don't shy away from a place because you have to share a bathroom. It's not like you're traveling in Mexico, after all. Here, you'll miss some really nice places and people (plus lower rates) if you refuse to share.

Some people envision "shared bath" very literally, as if there were five or six people in there all at once. Not the case, of course, and most often there are only two or three rooms sharing. And some of those might not be rented, in which case you'll end up with a private bath, anyway.

If you share, simply be courteous of other guests (translation: if you walk around naked at home, please throw on a robe here). Also, a sink in the bedroom can be a big help; then teeth can be brushed without having to get in the shared bathroom.

...Smoking: As more non-smokers are asserting themselves, more innkeepers are feeling less guilty and "just say no." Some inns allow smoking outside on porches only. Others don't want smokers to bother other guests so smoking is allowed only in the private guest rooms. Still others don't want the liability of people smoking in bed and don't allow it in guest rooms.

If smoking is allowed and it bothers you, you may wish to ask innkeepers if they personally smoke and in what particular areas of the house smoking is allowed.

...Children: While some establishments welcome children, others are designed as weekend or special-event adult getaways. They are not set up for children of any age who may disturb other guests. Others simply don't have cribs or child-proof furnishings. Some may accept older children but require renting a separate room for them. On the other hand, even places that say "no children" may make an exception when they have room, so it doesn't hurt to ask.

...Pets: Even fewer lodgings will accept pets than will accept children. Still, there are those that will. Many innkeepers will make arrangements for your pet at a local kennel at your request. Also, note that many innkeepers have their own pets, most of which are friendly animals that are thrilled to welcome guests.

...Other/Group Uses: Nearly every B&B will give you a price break for "whole house" rental for reunions, for instance. Other specialties are noted here.

...Driving Time/Directions: This section probably won't be helpful unless or until you are looking at a map or are in town trying to find the place. Driving times are approximate and will vary depending on starting points, road conditions and driving speed. Expect them to be reasonably accurate within a half-hour for summer driving.

...Deposit: Most innkeepers want a deposit to hold advance reservations. Ask about cancellation policies when making the reservation.

...Payment: Nearly every innkeeper will accept personal checks, so credit cards are not necessary. Small B&Bs often cannot afford the service charges tacked on by credit card companies, so they prefer to operate on a cash basis.

For more information, simply ask! This book provides an introduction to the innkeepers. Just pick up the phone and call. They'll be happy to help you.

Happy traveling!

Chatsworth B&B

984 Ashland   Owner/Operator:
St. Paul, MN 55104   Donna Gustafson
612-227-4288

When most of Donna and Earl Gustafson's eight children and assorted exchange students had left the nest, their three-story Victorian home in the Summit Hill neighborhood seemed awfully big and empty. Three years and many months of complete remodeling later, they found themselves in an apartment upstairs from a five-bedroom B&B.

"We wanted to stay here and we found one way we could do it," Donna said. "I really got the idea when I was looking with a group of friends for a yoga center." The realtor showing them big, older homes suggested using some of the rooms for a B&B to help finance the center. The yoga center never opened, "but the idea stuck." Chatsworth B&B opened February '86.

The house, built in 1902, had but one bathroom, so Donna and Earl looked at other homes to open a B&B. When they decided to turn their large closets into bathrooms, they were delighted to stay in their own home and have a B&B, too. Gustafsons are the fourth owners and one of the smallest families to live there, with only eight children. The second owners had 13 and the third owners had 10 children.

Guests may use the huge living room and fireplace, where the original stained glass is still in the windows. Breakfast is served in the polished birch dining room or can be eaten outside on a porch.

Rooms and Rates: Five - All on the second floor. The largest has private marble bath with double whirlpool and four-poster, lace canopy bed - $85. African-Asian room is done in rattan and wicker with porch, private bath with corner double whirlpool - $85. The other bedrooms share a bath (limited to four persons sharing) with a deep Japanese-style soaking tub, which fills up to the shoulders. Oriental room is in rose, green and black with oriental four-poster bed - $52. Scandinavian room has blue, rose and white twin beds (or king) with down comforters - $58. Victorian room has antique bed - $52. Add tax. Rates are double. Single $10 less. Extra person in room, $8.

Meals: Breakfast is served in the dining room and usually includes juice, coffee, tea, fresh fruits, muffins, breads, yogurt and granola.

Dates open: Year 'round   **Smoking:** No

Children: Check with owner   **Pets:** No

Other/Group Uses: Out-of-town wedding guests, reunions, small meetings, retreats.

Nearby: Governor's Residence and historic Summit Avenue homes, 2 blocks. Grand Avenue shops, restaurants, bus line to downtown St. Paul, 3 blocks. Several colleges nearby (William Mitchell, Macalester, St. Thomas).

Directions: Exit I-94, go south on Lexington to Ashland, left two blocks to corner of Chatsworth. House is on right.

Deposit: First night's lodging

Payment: Cash, personal or traveler's checks only

Yoerg House

215 W. Isabel St.   Owners/Operators:
St. Paul, MN 55107   Kathy and Jack Kohrer
612-224-9436

Kathy and Jack Kohrer discovered a "for sale" sign in front of this riverbluff home while taking a leisurely drive through St. Paul, looking at houses for sale for someone else.

Built in 1875, the French Second Empire home they stumbled onto was a real "find." It was designed by architect Monroe Sheire, who built the house of territorial governor Alexander Ramsey, now open for tours by Minnesota Historical Society. The stenciled burlap walls, hand-painted murals, 12-foot ceilings, oak woodwork and leaded glass remained.

Only two other people had owned the home since Elovina and Anthony Yoerg, the Bavarian immigrants who started a family brewery on the other side of the river. When the brewery moved across the river, so did the owners, building this home. The remains of the brewery walls can be seen in the ravine below the house. The brewery was closed in about 1956 and Yoerg beer is no longer made.

Kathy, a flight attendant, and Jack, a food service director, bought the home in June 1986, thinking "someday, a B&B might be fun," Kathy said. By the fall of 1987 the B&B was open after replumbing, rewiring, stripping woodwork, removing plaster walls and insulating, adding a huge bathroom and redecorating. Downstairs, they preserved the unusual hand-painted murals in the dining room and stenciling elsewhere, and the home is a candidate for the National Register of Historic Places.

Guests are welcome to put their drinks in the refrigerator and they have the use of the living room, parlor and front porch. Two more guest rooms with private baths are planned for mid-1989.

Rooms and Rates: Three - All upstairs with ceiling fans and terry bathrobes in the closet. They share two baths, one a former bedroom with shower and separate clawfoot tub, the other with a clawfoot tub with shower. Marlette's Room has a queen white iron bed, fainting couch, hand-stitched lace spread. Elovina's Room has a double bed, antique oriental rugs and a view of the Capitol. Annie's Room has two twin brass beds and it overlooks downtown St. Paul. $55, tax included. Rates are single or double.

Meals: Continental breakfast is served in the dining room at a time arranged the night before and includes fresh-squeezed juice, muffins, seasonal fruit and hot or cold cereal.

Dates open: Year 'round

Smoking: Not in guest rooms

Children: 14 and older

Pets: No (dog and cats on premises)

Other/Group Uses: Small business meetings or gatherings (pocket doors close off dining room).

Nearby: Downtown St. Paul (Ordway Music Hall, Science Museum of Minnesota, Civic Center, World Trade Center, shopping and restaurants), 4 minutes. Downtown Minneapolis, airport, Minnesota Zoo, within 20 minutes.

Directions: Located on the west side of St. Paul on the riverbluff overlooking downtown. Talk with innkeepers for specific directions. Map sent.

Deposit: First night's lodging

Payment: Cash, personal or traveler's checks only

Evelo's B&B

2301 Bryant Ave. S.   Owners/Operators:
Minneapolis, MN 55405   Sheryl and David Evelo
612-374-9656

Located in Minneapolis' Lowry Hill East neighborhood, this three-story home was built in 1897 for Dr. John and Kate Bell. It has had several subsequent owners, including the nearby "Miss Woods School."

"It was a dorm for about 20 years for the 'Miss Woods girls'," said Sheryl. The school was for nursery and early elementary school teacher training, and up to 25 women lived here, taking meals elsewhere.

The Evelos, both of whom are teachers in Minneapolis, bought the home in 1972 and started a B&B in 1979, believed to be the first B&B in Minnesota. "We traveled in Europe and stayed in B&Bs and we thought it was fun and interesting and a nice way to travel," Sheryl said. "The first year, I think we had one room and two guests." But publicity in the Minneapolis paper gave them a boost. Guests now include tourists, families visiting relatives in the area, students, actors, artists and businesspeople.

Downstairs, the living room, dining room and screened-in front porch are "public." The first floor is done in heavy dark oak millwork and lit with antique art glass lamps. The furnishings are turn-of-the-century antiques Sheryl and David have collected.

One guest room (the former maid's room) is on the second floor, and the other three rooms are on the third. Guests use the maid's stairway and have a key. A small refrigerator, coffeemaker and phone are on the third floor landing, and portable TVs are available.

Rooms and Rates: Four - All share bath with tub only on third floor, and second bath is available on first floor. All rooms are doubles, and one has an extra twin bed; rollaways are available. $25 single, $35 double, $45 triple. Add tax.

Meals: Breakfast is served in the dining room. Evelos are up early to buy fresh bread at small neighborhood bakeries. No meat is served. Menu may include Sherry's Egg Bake (eggs, mushrooms and cheese), fresh fruit, breads or muffins, coffee, tea and juice.

Dates open: Year 'round   **Smoking:** No

Children: Yes (crib, highchair available)   **Pets:** No

Other/Group Uses: No

Nearby: Many restaurants within walking or bus distance. Guthrie Theatre and Walker Art Institute, Lake of the Isles, 6 blocks. Minneapolis Institute of Art and Children's Theatre, 11 blocks. Uptown-Calhoun Square, 8 blocks. Bus to downtown, 1 block (or a 20-minute walk to downtown).

Directions: Exit from I-94 onto Hennepin Avenue South. Turn left on 22nd Street (second stoplight), then right on Bryant (two blocks from light).

Deposit: First night's lodging

Payment: Cash, personal or traveler's checks only

Linné Bed & Breakfast

2645 Fremont Ave. S.
Minneapolis, MN 55408
612-377-4418

Owners/Operators:
Casey Higgins and
Robert Torsten Eriksson

In 1896 when Minneapolis master builder Theron P. Healy contracted with Swedish carpenters to build this home, it cost $3,000, fine craftsmanship and all. In just seven years, when Healy was again called in by the owners to build an addition, the extra room alone cost $1,000. Already, the home was in a popular part of the city. Today, it's within walking distance of some of Minneapolis' best-liked restaurants, shopping and night spots, plus the lakes and theaters.

That's one reason why Casey Higgins and Robert Torsten Eriksson wanted to live here. (In fact, Casey sold her car when they moved into this home and she walks to shopping and work.) That's also why they thought it'd be a good spot for a metropolitan B&B, welcoming business travelers and visitors.

"We had been out to the Finger Lakes of New York and stayed in inns and B&Bs," said Robert. "This would be a way to have an old house like this and keep it up, and be able to share it with other people." "We are both cooks and nurses -- 'service people,' " Casey said, so they knew they'd like the hospitality industry.

The home was in good shape in January 1987 when they moved in. They set to work to decorate the guest rooms on the second floor in Scandinavian style, as a tribute to Robert's Swedish grandparents and because they had lived and traveled there (the B&B is named for the pink-and-white Swedish flower called "twinflower" here). They opened three rooms in May 1987, and the rooms are mostly white, with prints, tapestries or weavings. Swedish mineral water and truffles are found in the rooms, and Swedish pancakes usually are on the weekend breakfast menu.

The house has family heirlooms and antiques. Guests are welcome to use the living room fireplace and the library. Off-street parking is behind the house.

Rooms and Rates: Three - All upstairs with window air conditioners and ceiling fans. All share bath with wood-rimmed clawfoot tub with shower. #1 has a queen iron and brass bed. #2 has queen brass bed, bentwood chairs and table, shuttered windows. #3 has pencil post four-poster bed, rose accents, wainscotted sun porch with wicker furniture. $60 weekends, $50 weekdays, single or double. Add tax. No third person in room. Long-term business discounts.

Meals: Breakfast is served weekdays by 9 a.m. to guest rooms, in the parlor or in the dining room, and it includes fresh muffins or scones, fruit or fresh-squeezed juice, Swedish flatbread, cheese and preserves. On Saturday and Sunday, it also includes an egg dish, bacon or sausage, or Swedish pancakes.

Dates open: Year 'round   **Smoking:** No

Children: Over 11   **Pets:** No

Other/Group Uses: Holiday parties and special events.

Nearby: Comedy clubs, bus line to downtown, 1 block. Uptown (restaurants, bakeries, shops, movies), 4 blocks. Lake of the Isles, 4 blocks. Lake Calhoun, 6 blocks. Guthrie Theater, Minneapolis Institute of Arts, 11 blocks.

Directions: From I-94, take Hennepin Ave. exit (south). From Hennepin, turn left on 27th St. to Fremont (1 block). Turn right on Fremont.

Deposit: First night's lodging or confirmation by credit card

Payment: Cash, personal or traveler's checks or AMEX

Nicollet Island Inn

95 Merriam
Minneapolis, MN 55401
612-331-1800

Owners:
Isle West Associates
General Manager: Marilyn Sapp

Nicollet Island has been located in the hub of downtown activity since the founding of the city itself at nearby St. Anthony Falls. The small island in between the main stream of the Mississippi River and a side channel was crossed with railroad tracks and was a warehouse, factory and residential district.

Today, the island slowly is undergoing a renaissance. Former row houses and some homes have been renovated and the Minneapolis Park Board has added a band pavillion and park on the island, just a block or two from an historic bridge leading to Main Street and its RiverPlace shopping center.

And business travelers seeking more individualized and personal accommodations than large downtown hotels can offer and couples looking for a city getaway are frequenting this small hotel smack dab in the middle of the city.

The Nicollet Island Inn is in a limestone building on the southeast side of the island. It was built in 1893 as the Island Sash and Door factory. During its construction, it withstood a major fire that demolished most of the other businesses on the island. It was once surrounded by other island factories and businesses including Minnesota Bee Supply Co., a coffin and lumber company, and the William Bros. Boiler Works.

Earlier in this decade, the building was renovated as an inn, but the owners filed bankruptcy and it sat empty for more than a year. In June 1988, Isle West Associates, the new owners, opened the inn after adding new carpeting and wallpaper, moving the bar up from the basement level to riverside, and making other remodeling changes. Guests now can order room service, ride to their rooms in a glass elevator, and enjoy gourmet dining for three meals a day.

Rooms and Rates: 24 - All with queen or king beds, color TVs and VCR (complimentary movies at desk), hairdryers, individually decorated with antique reproductions. Examples include #203 corner suite, four-poster bed, large whirlpool with heavy terry robes, done in greens - $90. #312 has king white iron and brass bed, done in blues and cream, handicapped accessible - $80. River view rooms $85. Add tax. Corporate discounts and weekend packages.

Meals: Three meals a day served in restaurant. Adjoining Nic's on the Island bar also serves food. Breakfast for two included in weekend packages, served either in bed or in the restaurant.

Dates open: Year 'round   **Smoking:** 2 rooms non-smoking

Children: Yes (rollaways available)   **Pets:** No

Other/Group Uses: Meetings, weddings, banquets, anniversaries, 18 to 175 people in three basement banquet rooms.

Nearby: RiverPlace shopping and restaurants, historic Main Street leading to St. Anthony Falls, just across historic bridge over Mississippi River. Nicollet Island Park and pavillion, 1/2 block.

Directions: Follow Hennepin Ave. north from downtown over the Mississippi, turn right just over the river before RiverPlace, turn right again in one block over historic bridge to inn.

Deposit: Confirmation by credit card

Payment: Cash, personal or traveler's checks, VISA, MasterCard, AMEX, Diners Club or Discover

Christopher Inn

201 Mill St.
Excelsior, MN 55331
612-474-6816

Owners/Operators:
Joan and Howard Johnson
Innkeeper: Cheryl Louden

A contractor, C.F. Warner, desïgned and built this Victorian mansion in 1887, but he couldn't find a buyer when he wanted to sell it five years later. A Minneapolis resident, James Wyer, simply traded homes with Warner. There's no telling how Warner did in the deal, but Wyer made out like a bandit. This home's front lawn then stretched two blocks to the shore of Lake Minnetonka, the perfect place for his large family.

In 1930, the house was sold to the Pearce family, which never lived in it but rented it as a duplex. It was turned into office space in 1977. In 1985, after just one night in a B&B, Joan and Howard Johnson decided that's the type of business they'd do well and enjoy. The house was for sale; they found investors; and after less than three months of major restoration and modernization, they opened the inn in July 1985.

During the process, five bathrooms, a commercial kitchen, and a handicapped access ramp were added. New plumbing and furnace, exterior painting, new furniture and restoring original woodwork was necessary, and "every room had to be painted or wallpapered," said Howard.

Today, the inn is on the National Register of Historic Places. It has a spacious screened porch, plenty of working fireplaces, including one that burns in the dining room at breakfast, and what is believed to be the state's only grass tennis court. Guests are welcome to use it and the inn's bicycles.

During three seasons, a horse-drawn carriage is available to take guests to nearby restaurants. An afternoon tea is scheduled when the inn is full to allow guests to socialize.

Rooms and Rates: Seven - Named for Johnson family members, and the Library. It has handicapped access and an antique hidden Murphy bed and shares a full bath with the dining room - $65. Other examples include Ann's Room, which has two twin beds, is done in cranberry, has sink in the room, shared bath - $70. David's Room has a table by the window, queen bed, working fireplace, private bath with shower - $110. Add tax. Rates single or double. Off-season midweek and business discounts.

28

Meals: Breakfast is open to guests first, at about 8:30 a.m., then to the public by reservation only. It may include homemade breads, juice, coffee, granola, fresh fruit, plus varied entrees of seafood omelettes, seafood strata casserole, peaches and cream French toast, and Swedish apple pancakes.

Dates open: Year 'round

Smoking: In designated areas

Children: In some rooms

Pets: No

Other/Group Uses: Weddings and receptions to 250, with special wedding packages, including catering, music, flowers, photos, tents and carriage.

Nearby: Two restaurants, 1 block. City Park and swimming, 4 blocks. Antique shops, downtown Excelsior, paddlewheel boat rides, 2 blocks.

Driving Time/Directions from Twin Cities: Within 30 minutes. Take Highway 7 west to Excelsior. Turn left at the parking lot immediately over the bridge coming in to town.

Deposit: First night's lodging or confirmation by credit card

Payment: Cash, personal or traveler's checks, VISA, MasterCard or AMEX

Bluff Creek Inn

1161 Bluff Creek Drive
Chaska, MN 55318
612-445-2735

Owner/Operator:
Anne Karels

"Let me live in the house by the side of the road and be a friend to man," wrote S.W. Foss. Anne Karels is living those words at her B&B, an 1860 brick country home.

The land, off Highway 212 east of Chaska, was granted to Chaska pioneer Joseph Vogel by President Abraham Lincoln before Minnesota was a state. Over the years, some of the land went for the highway, some for the railroad; the barns have been torn down; the house was foreclosed during the Depression, divided into a duplex, and rented for several years.

Since then, many changes have been made, including putting in new plumbing, central air conditioning and a long front porch with swings at both ends, adding two bedrooms and restoring the summer kitchen. Ten rooms were wallpapered and woodwork was stripped. The B&B opened in June 1985, and Karels bought it in mid-1988.

She had decided a B&B was a good way to combine her business, "people" and culinary skills, but she hadn't planned on making the move so soon. "In fact, when my last employer asked in an interview what my long-term goals were, I told him I intended to own and operate a B&B within five yeras. Never did I dream that less than a year later I would be the innkeeper at Bluff Creek Inn!"

Guests enjoy the quiet atmosphere and swinging on the porch or tree swings. The house is carpeted and looks out over wildflowers. A three-course breakfast is served in the dining room in front of a roaring fire or in the summer kitchen where a pot belly stove keeps the room toasty in spring and fall.

Rooms: Five - Three rooms have their own water closets (toilet and sink) curtained off and share a clawfoot tub in a separate bathroom. Examples include Emma's Room, done in green, red and beige, double four-poster Civil War bed and Chaska brick wall - $65. Elizabeth's Room has a double, four-poster tester bed with Laura Ashley prints in green and rose; porch faces sunset, and private bath includes clawfoot tub - $85. Add tax. Rates are double. Single $5 less.

Meals: Breakfast is served in the dining room or on the summer porch at 9 a.m. and it may include fresh fruits and muffins, an entree such as puff pancakes or Eggs Florentine and a dessert. Dinners by prior arrangement.

Dates open: Year 'round

Smoking: On porches only

Children: Over 12 - ask innkeeper

Pets: No

Other/Group Uses: Weddings, groom's dinners, reunions, small business meetings, church groups and tours, couples cooking classes.

Nearby: Valley Fair, Canterbury Downs race track, Renaissance Festival, Murphy's Landing, Chanhassen Dinner Theater, Minnesota Landscape Arboretum, Carver Park Reserve and "494 Strip" all 10-15 minutes away.

Driving Time/Directions from Twin Cities: Within 30 minutes. I-494 to Highway 169/212. Turn right on first road on the right past Highway 101 junction. House is on left.

Deposit: Full amount

Payment: Cash, personal or traveler's checks, VISA or MasterCard

Sunny Morning Manor

314 S. Scott St.
Shakopee, MN 55379
612-496-1482

Owners/Operators:
Judy and Dennis Clausen

Built in 1880, this home had a massive entryway with stained glass and extensive egg-and-dart carved woodwork. It was fitting of the social position of its builder, H.B. Strait, a banker and Congressman with a long military career to boot.

But by 1986, when Judy and Dennis Clausen first saw it, it had lost much of its grandeur. The third owner, a widow with six children to support, had divided it into three apartments, closing off some parlors to use as walls. The most recent owners lived in one apartment but no longer rented the other two and closed them off. Years before, the wood siding had been covered by red tarpaper.

Still, Judy fell in love with it. "The first time we were in it it was all over," she said. In February 1987 they bought it, "wanting to do a B&B but not knowing if the city would give us a permit." They'd stayed in a B&B once and liked it. "We lived in the country on a lake and led a secluded, quiet life for eight years. Coming back, we decided to do something different with our home." The city did grant the permit, but there was much to be done before the B&B could open.

For starters, there was no central furnace -- each of the three apartments was heated by separate stoves. New plumbing and wiring was needed. The back end of the house was gutted and a new, large kitchen was built there. Judy pulled up the old linoleum covering the dining room floor to reveal to a very surprised Dennis a picture frame parquet floor hidden underneath. The Clausen family did much of the work themselves, including redecorating with new wallpaper and furniture, stressing comfort and use, not period style, Judy noted. The woodwork downstairs needed only minimal refinishing.

The living room with TV is open to guests, and they can help themselves to coffee in the kitchen. Upstairs, a common sitting area has a TV as well.

Rooms and Rates: Three - All upstairs with handmade quilts, sharing a bath with clawfoot tub and separate shower, decorated with wainscotting. Room 1 has queen-sized waterbed, done in greens and tan - $60. Room 2 has double white iron bed, floral wallpaper in blues and rose - $50. Room 3 has double bed, sitting area with separate stove, done in pink and cream florals - $50. Add tax. Single $10 less. Extra person in room, $10.

Meals: Breakfast is served in the dining room at a time arranged the night before and it may include a baked Finnish pancake, sausage and scrambled eggs, fresh fruit with whipped cream, and juice, coffee or milk.

Dates open: Year 'round   **Smoking:** In designated areas

Children: Yes (cots and cribs available)   **Pets:** No

Other/Group Uses: "Not yet."

Nearby: Canterbury Downs race track, Valley Fair amusement park, Murphy's Landing restored historic village, Renaissance Festival (fall weekends), restaurants, within 3 miles. Chanhassen Dinner Theater, 10 miles.

Driving Time/Directions from Twin Cities: Within 30 minutes. I-35W to Hwy. 13 exit, west to Shakopee. Hwy. 169 west through stoplight at Hwy. 101 three blocks to Scott St. Turn left (south) two blocks; house is across from school.

Deposit: First night's lodging or confirmation by credit card

Payment: Cash, personal or traveler's checks, VISA and MasterCard

Hazelwood

705 Vermillion
Hastings, MN 55033
612-437-3297

Owners/Operators:
Pam and Dick Thorsen

Judge John Heinen would be remembered as one of the youngest men ever to be elected as Hastings' mayor. He would also be remembered as the father of eight, one of whom was said to be the first person to cross the town's new spiral bridge.

But many would remember him best for his electric stove. The Judge purchased the town's first electric cooking stove, which drew many spectators. But to see the new-fangled invention, other prospective cooks and buyers had to go to the garage. The Judge had the stove hooked up there to a separate electric meter. Then he monitored the electricity needed when his wife cooked various foods. After a month of recordkeeping, he gave the OK to move it inside the house.

The Judge's house, built in 1890, had another focal point still prominent today -- a large, thick, curved corner window. Children called it "the circus window" because when they stood in front of it, it made them taller and thinner.

It was perhaps the woodwork, though, that took in Pam and Dick Thorsen. The entryway has ornate oak arches. Sycamore, Georgia pine and other wood is found throughout. It was remodeled into a law office by attorney Tim Moratzka. In August 1988, Moratzka was moving his practice and wanted to sell. "He called us because he knew we knew people who were interested in old houses, " Pam said.

With the River Rose, Thorsen's second B&B, still three months away from opening and stripped to its walls, they didn't think they'd be interested in a third B&B. "I said to Dick, 'Maybe we should just look at it.' " The renovated house, in excellent shape and with only redecorating and furnishing needed, appealed to them. After analyzing the business potential, an arrangement was reached. A November 1988 opening was planned. It's named for Hazel Jacobsen, the town's tireless historian, who has researched and promoted Hastings since 1945.

Rooms and Rates: Four - All with private baths with tubs and showers. Three guest rooms on second floor, one with double bed, two with queen beds - $45 and $55. Suite on third floor has queen bed, day bed - $85. Add tax. Packages for two-night minimum required on weekends with Friday night light supper and Saturday night five-course dinner with chamber music included, served at the River Rose. Weekday package available with limo service to local restaurants.

Meals: Breakfast is served in the dining room, on the porch or to guest rooms at a time arranged the night before. It includes fresh fruit, an egg and meat dish, pastries, coffee, tea and juice. Friday night light supper and Saturday night five-course dinner are required with weekend packages and served at the River Rose, two blocks away. Other meals by special arrangement.

Dates open: Year 'round   **Smoking:** On porch only

Children: Talk with innkeeper   **Pets:** No

Other/Group Uses: Conferences, meetings and other uses combined with the River Rose and Thorwood.

Nearby: Downtown Hastings shops and restaurants, 5 blocks. Walking tour, parks, lock and dam, nature center, ski areas, fishing and boating, winery.

Driving Time/Directions from Twin Cities: Within 30 minutes. Highway 61 south to Hastings. Inn is on southeast corner of the highway (Vermillion Street) and 7th Street.

Deposit: First night's lodging or confirmation by credit card

Payment: Cash, personal or traveler's checks, VISA, MasterCard or AMEX

The River Rose

620 Ramsey   Owners/Operators:
Hastings, MN 55033   Pam and Dick Thorsen
612-437-3297   Innkeeper: Marjorie Bush

When, in 1986, the City of Hastings declared this National Register building surplus property and requested proposals for its sale and future use, Thorsens could hardly refuse to send an "entry." The 1880 building had so much in common with Thorwood, their seven guest-room inn, that expanding to it seemed fated.

The River Rose was built in the same year as Thorwood by Rudolph Latto, the friend of the builder of Thorwood, William Thompson. The curving stairway at the entrance is the same, as is other woodwork, presumably from Thompson's lumber yard. The River Rose also served as one of Hastings' hospitals, as did Thorwood. Latto ended up leaving the house to the City for use as a hospital, and gave $10,000 so one bed always would be free of charge for the needy.

Rudolph and Marie Latto's home had come after many years of work. When the Austrian immigrants first came to Hastings, Marie had a shack on the bank of the Mississippi where she cooked meals for the lumbermen guiding logs downriver. Rudolph worked as a stableman at the hotel and other jobs before becoming vice-president of the German-American National Bank.

Latto's generous gift of the hospital was used until the community hospital was built in 1953. Then the city leased it as a board and care home. When requests for proposals went out in 1986, major work on the building was needed. Thorsens' new B&B was one of three proposals. Dick and a crew of eight have done major restoration, everything from new furnaces and air conditioning on down.

Rooms and Rates: Six - All with queen-sized beds and private baths. All except Isabelle's Room have double whirlpools and fireplaces. Examples include: Isabelle's Room has iron bed, sitting porch, wicker swing, bath with shower only - $65. Rebecca's Suite has separate bathing area with fireplace; large sunporch bedroom with fireplace, brass and iron bed, done in greens and ivory - $150. Mississippi Suite is on third floor, has separate living, bathing and sleeping rooms, plus porch with gingerbread. Glass wall on stairwell, baby grand piano, copper soaking tub plus whirlpool, automatic table comes up from floor, canopied bed - $250. Add tax. Packages for two-night minimum required on weekends with Friday night light supper and Saturday night five-course dinner with chamber music included. Weekday packages available with limo service to local restaurants.

36

Meals: Breakfast is served at a time arranged the night before in one of two parlors, in the dining room, library, on porches or to the guest room. It includes fresh fruit, an egg and meat dish, pastries, coffee, tea and juice. Friday night light supper and Saturday night five-course dinner required with weekend packages. Other meals by special arrangement.

Dates open: Year 'round   **Smoking:** On porches only

Children: Talk with innkeeper   **Pets:** No

Other/Group Uses: Small conferences, weddings, groom's dinners, retreats, ladies' PJ parties, Victorian high teas.

Nearby: Downtown Hastings shops and restaurants, 3 blocks. Walking tour, parks, lock and dam, nature center, ski areas, fishing and boating, winery.

Driving Time/Directions from Twin Cities: Within 30 minutes.
Highway 61 south to Hastings, turn left on Seventh St. to corner. Inn is on left.

Deposit: First night's lodging or confirmation by credit card

Payment: Cash, personal or traveler's checks, VISA, MasterCard or AMEX

Thorwood B&B Inn

Fourth and Pine
Hastings, MN 55033
612-437-3297

Owners/Operators:
Pam and Dick Thorsen

William and Sara Thompson originally had this mansion built in 1880. Thompson was a wealthy owner of a lumber company on the Mississippi River at Hastings, just before it meets the St. Croix River.

Thompson's daughter, Kate, inherited the house, where she lived with her riverboat husband, Captain Anthony. The home was purchased in 1929 by Dr. Herman A. Fasbender, who converted it to a private hospital. An elevator was added to the third floor operating room and second floor nursery; the pharmacy was on the first floor. The hospital operated, so to speak, until about 1951, when the community's Regina Hospital was built.

When Thorsens bought the building in 1979 and named it Thorwood, it had been a six-plex apartment house since the 1950s. "We bought it thinking this is a wonderful old house," Pam said. Thorsens took out walls, putting rooms back to original dimensions. It's on the National Register of Historic Places.

Thorwood opened with two rooms in February '83. Today, it has seven, and recent remodeling has meant fireplaces and double whirlpools were added in many rooms. Thorsens live in the separate servant's quarters and have since opened two other B&Bs in Hastings, the River Rose and Hazelwood.

Thorwood is decorated with period antiques and Victorian wallpaper. Every room has a teddy bear, courtesy of the Thorsen's two daughters. The downstairs parlor is a popular gathering place. Guests automatically receive an evening snack, but don't check out without saying goodbye - a last surprise awaits.

Rooms and Rates: Seven - All with private bath and central air, $65, $85 or $125. Examples include: Capt. Anthony's Room has a queen brass canopy bed, a day bed, and is done in rose and teal blue, shower only - $65. The Lullaby Room, the former nursery, is done in peach and grey, queen bed, double whirlpool - $85. Sara's Room has a queen bed in a loft and a double whirlpool below - $125. Steeple Room has a see-through fireplace, queen bed and double whirlpool in the steeple - $125. Add tax. Commercial rates. Packages for two-night minimum required on weekends with Friday night light supper and Saturday night five-course dinner with chamber music included, served at the River Rose. Weekday package available with limo service to local restaurants.

Meals: Breakfast is served in the dining room, on one of the porches or in a huge basket to the guest room door. It may include platters of oven omelettes, hot pastries, sausages, muffins, fresh fruit, coffee, tea and juice. Evening snack is local wine or catawba, fruit, pastries. Victorian picnics available.

Dates open: Year 'round　　　　　　　**Pets:** No

Children: Talk with innkeepers　　　　**Smoking:** No

Other/Group Uses: Small reunions, business retreats, mystery weekends, groom's dinners.

Nearby: Downtown Hastings is a Main Street USA town, 4 blocks. Walking tour between Thorwood and downtown. Levee Park, Lake Rebecca, Lock and Dam #2, fishing and boating. Two ski areas, nature center.

Driving Time/Directions from Twin Cities: Within 30 minutes.
Highway 61 south to Hastings, right on Fourth to Pine. Thorwood is on right.

Deposit: First night's lodging or confirmation by credit card

Payment: Cash, personal or traveler's checks, VISA, MasterCard or AMEX

The Afton House Inn

P.O. Box 326
Afton, MN 55001
612-436-8883

Owners/Operators:
Kathy and Gordy Jarvis
Manager: Judy Alberg

Thirty years after the first French families settled in Afton, Charles Cushing built the Cushing Hotel. The 1867 hotel opening was the second for the village of Afton; the Paterson's Hotel already had burned to the ground.

In 1907, Mary "Ma" Pennington became the owner, and the hotel's reputation as a restaurant was born. "Ma" served Sunday chicken dinners which were famous for miles around. The chickens were raised out in back of the restaurant, and diners knew they couldn't get anything fresher.

Over the years, other owners continued to run and expand the restaurant, but the hotel faded out. In 1976, it was purchased by Gordy and Kathy Jarvis. Gordy was chef/manager of McGuire's restaurant and Twins Motor Inn. "We wanted to bring it back to its original use, and there was a need in the area for a hotel," Gordy said. Thus began a seven-year challenge to secure needed permits for the building, listed on the National Register of Historic Places.

Finally, from Oct. 1, 1985, to April 1, 1986, the hotel was restored. The building was floodproofed and the upper floors were essentially gutted and rebuilt. New wiring, plumbing, and other major work was necessary, down to new brick sidewalks. An addition allowed the inn to have 12 rooms, instead of the original eight, and groups can be accommodated.

The hotel re-opened April 7, 1986, with the granddaughter of "Ma" Pennington present at the ceremonies. A whirlpool room, fireplace and tanning beds are available to guests.

Rooms and Rates: 12 - All with private baths and TVs, each decorated differently with antiques and reproductions in "country" wallpapers. Examples include #26 with a double iron and brass bed - $55. #29 with a four-poster bed and a deck overlooking the marina and St. Croix River - $85. #32 with king bed, done in rose - $75. All rates are $50, $55, $75, $85, and $100 doubles. Add tax. Extra person in room, $8. Midweek and winter discounts; lodging and ski packages.

Meals: Continental breakfast included Sunday through Thursday nights. Three meals available in dining rooms or Catfish saloon (sandwiches). Sunday brunch.

Dates open: Year 'round   **Smoking:** 3 rooms non-smoking

Children: Yes (no charge for cribs)   **Pets:** No

Other/Group Uses: Weddings, rehearsal dinners, meetings and seminars with food service, boat cruises on the St. Croix River, senior citizen luncheon tours.

Nearby: St. Croix River marinas and dockage, gift shops, ice cream parlor, toy shop, 1-2 blocks. Afton State Park, 3 miles. Downhill and x-c skiing, 2-4 miles.

Driving Time/Directions from Twin Cities: Within 30 minutes. I-94 east to Highway 95, south four miles to Afton, continue straight on County Rd. 21 when 95 turns to right. Inn is on the left at the corner.

Deposit: First night's lodging or confirmation by credit card

Payment: Cash, personal or traveler's checks, VISA, MasterCard or AMEX

Stillwater

Lowell Inn

102 N. Second
Stillwater, MN 55082
612-439-1100

Owners/Operators:
Maureen and Arthur Palmer

Arthur Palmer was literally born into innkeeping. His parents, Nelle and Arthur, Sr., opened the Lowell Inn under their management on Christmas Day 1930, and it has remained in the family since. Nelle had been one of the Obrecht Sisters, a family acting company, and she met and married pianist Arthur while traveling the Midwest as they produced live theater. Tired of living on the road and concerned about their future as talking movies became popular, they jumped at the chance to manage the Lowell Inn.

Adding little touches of collectibles and antiques helped draw guests on the back roads to the faraway village of Stillwater. In 1945, the Palmers were able to purchase the inn. While both his parents have passed on, Art Palmer and Maureen, his wife, have raised most of their nine children on innkeeping traditions.

Originally, Stillwater's lumber barons wheeled and dealed in the Sawyer House, a luxury hotel built in 1848. It was demolished in 1924 in order to build the Lowell Inn. The Williamsburg design is said to resemble Mount Vernon and the original 13 colonies are represented with flags and 13 white pillars. Change at the Lowell Inn will continue: Palmer plans to fill the entire block with a complex of additional rooms and meeting facilities.

Rooms and Rates: 21 - All on the second and third floors, with private baths, complimentary bar or wine, and a ceramic cat on the bed; most done in opulent provincial antiques or reproductions, with a stereo system. Four bridal/anniversary rooms have round double whirlpools - $139. Four bridal/anniversary rooms have round showers - $129. Six have king beds - $109. Four have queen beds - $99. Two are called "petite double," though the lavender room is big - $89. The Nelle Suite has a living room and an inlaid games board, queen bed - $139. Rates single or double. Add tax. American Plan, including dinner and breakfast, available.

Meals: Lunch and dinner available in dining rooms (no room service).

Dates open: Year 'round   **Smoking:** Yes

Children: Talk with innkeepers   **Pets:** No

Other/Group Uses: Talk with innkeepers.

Nearby: Downtown Stillwater gift shops, restaurants, winery, antique shops, 1-4 blocks. St. Croix River, 3 blocks.

Driving Time/Directions from Twin Cities: Within 30 minutes.
Highway 36 east to Stillwater, follow signs to downtown. Turn left on Myrtle at third stoplight, go 1 block to Second St., turn right. Inn is on left.

Deposit: Full amount

Payment: Cash, personal or traveler's checks, VISA, MasterCard, AMEX or Diners Club

Overlook Inn

210 E. Laurel St.   Owners/Operators:
Stillwater, MN 55082   Janel and David Belz
612-439-3409

Janel and David Belz thought they'd get into the B&B business slowly, opening just one room in 1987 in a Stillwater mansion. The building, a 10,000-square-foot beauty named the Sauntry Mansion, was what drew people. "People were interested in it -- it was a way to share the house," said Janel.

Soon after, a smaller Stillwater home became available, and Belzes jumped at the chance to open four guests rooms. Located on 2.5 acres, this home had something the huge mansion did not -- an outstanding view of the St. Croix River.

Part of the Overlook Inn was built in 1859 by Judge Hollis Murdock when he settled in Stillwater from New York to practice law. His law office was also in the home on the first floor, complete with built-in safe. In 1870, when he became a probate judge, he added the back half of the house.

Murdock's widow sold the home in 1911 to the man who headed up the shoe factory in the first state prison, located just down the hill. Then the Comfort family bought it. Mildred Comfort wrote the best-selling children's books, the "Peter and Nancy" series, but her books were not yet popular and she lost the house. In 1925, the Peterson family bought the empty house and owned it for the next 60 years. The law office portion was then used as a print shop.

Belzes have discovered an old shaft on the property, apparently used as part of the Underground Railroad, shelter for blacks hiding from rivertown bounty hunters.

Today, Belzes have restored and renovated, adding baths and a "comfortable Victorian" decor. In the winter, hors d'oeuvres are served in the evening by the fireplace in one of two parlors; a 1890s baby grand is in the other parlor. Florists by trade, Belzes named the guest rooms after flowers.

Rooms and Rates: Four - All with queen beds and ceiling fans. Queen Anne Suite on the main floor suite is the former law office, with fireplace and built-in woodwork, private bath with shower only - $95. Rosebud Room has lace spread, done in deep rose colors, shares bath in hall with six-foot tub only, plus bath on main floor with shower - $75. Magnolia Room has brass bed, done in peach, greens and white - $65. Gardenia Suite has French doors overlooking the river, sitting area, done in greens and florals, private bath with shower only - $95. Rates are single or double. Add tax.

Meals: Breakfast is served in the dining room or on the screened porch at 9:30 a.m. and includes homemade baked goods, fruits, cheeses, juice and coffee. Picnic lunches packed. Special dinners prepared by request, can be served in the suites.

Dates open: Year 'round

Smoking: Only on porch

Children: No

Pets: No

Other/Group Uses: Small weddings, rehearsal dinners, reunions, showers and other special gatherings, with floral, photography and food service arranged.

Nearby: Minnesota Zephyr dining train, 106 steps down the hill. Andiamo paddlewheel on the St. Croix, downtown shops and restaurants, 4 blooks.

Driving Time/Directions from Twin Cities: Within 30 minutes.
Highway 36 east to downtown, go up hill at Myrtle to Second. Turn right, go past the city park. Inn is right next door on the river side of the street.

Deposit: First night's lodging

Payment: Cash, personal or traveler's checks only

The Rivertown Inn

306 W. Olive St.
Stillwater, MN 55082
612-430-2955

Owners/Operators:
Chuck and Judy Dougherty

It took Judy and Chuck Doughtery longer to buy a pick-up truck than to purchase this nine-room inn on the corner of Fifth and Olive streets, high above the St. Croix River.

"I had a deep, dark desire to get out of the restaurant business," said Chuck, who was working in Ohio, where Judy was teaching. He was looking for a business of his own, one much smaller than an eight-restaurant chain. Relatives in this area found the Inn, called Doughterys, and about two weeks later it was theirs.

The home originally was built for the family of John O'Brien, one of Stillwater's most prosperous lumbermen. But over the years, such a large single-family home could not be maintained. In the 1940s, it became a tri-plex. It also was used as an emergency shelter for foster children and, later, a girl's group home.

In 1981, the Victorian mansion was once again a single-family home and it was turned into a B&B. Pieces of fireplaces, original chandeliers and woodwork were found in the carriage house, which were put back in the main house.

Chuck and Judy took over as live-in innkeepers in May 1987. The next winter, they shut down for five weeks, adding five bathrooms, four double whirlpools and a sprinkler system to the three-floor inn, plus putting up new wallpaper. Air conditioning is the next major project on the agenda, Chuck said.

Breakfasts are served around a huge dining room table that can seat 18. Judy and Chuck have baking experience and make the pastries themselves. On weekends, wine and cheese also is served during a social hour that starts about 5:30.

Guests have use of the first floor's parlors and dining rooms, a large screened porch with a wicker swing, and a gazebo in the yard. Doughertys will arrange pick-up service from the local marinas on the St. Croix.

Rooms and Rates: Nine - All with private bath in room or down the hall, $45-$115. Examples include Julie's Room, done in blue and white, double bed, with corner whirlpool - $90. Faith's Room, the bridal suite, is done in peach and blue, 12-foot high lace canopy bed, fireplace - $115. Patricia's Room has high oak double bed, giant whirlpool, done in greens and peaches - $95. Add tax. Sunday through Thursday discounts.

Meals: Weekend breakfast is a buffet served 8:30-10:30 a.m. in the dining room, on the porch, or brought to the guest rooms. It includes meat and cheeses, more than a dozen home-baked pastries, fresh fruit, juice and coffee. Weekdays, guests receive a full breakfast.

Dates open: Year 'round   **Smoking:** On porches only

Children: If under 12, check with owner   **Pets:** No

Other/Group Uses: Meetings, weddings, showers and reunions of up to 20 people. Luncheons, teas and dinners catered by the Doughertys.

Nearby: Downtown shops, restaurants, caves, antique shops, 4 blocks. St. Croix River with Andiamo paddlewheel cruise, 5 blocks.

Driving Time/Directions from Twin Cities: Within 30 minutes.
Highway 36 east to downtown Stillwater, turn left on Olive Street (the second street after the first stoplight). Go up hill to Fifth. Inn is on the corner.

Deposit: Full amount

Payment: Cash, personal or traveler's checks, VISA or MasterCard

Marine on the St. Croix

Asa Parker House

17500 St. Croix Trail N.　　　　　Owner/Operator:
Marine on the St. Croix, MN 54047　　Ivonne Cuendet
612-433-5248

When Ivonne Cuendet opened her B&B in July 1986, the plumber was barely on his way out when guests were on their way in. Work was done at breakneck speed between May 1 and the July 18 arrival of guests, who wanted to hold a family reunion in her B&B. "They told me I had contributed to their memories, and I thought, 'Oh, this *is* like a Walton house,' " she said, referring to the TV Walton family's closeness.

The compliment on the hominess of this 1856 building by her first guests was heady stuff for Cuendet, who has thought about running a B&B for years and finally took the plunge alone in late 1985. "I always had the sense that if the right house came around I should do it."

Originally, the "right house" was built by Asa Parker, the Vermont lumberman who brought the lumber industry up the St. Croix River from Stillwater. He and Isabella, his wife, had servants, and Cuendet now lives in those servants' quarters. His house was modeled after a stately Vermont home.

Cuendet is the fifth owner of the home, which is in Marine's National Historic District. An 88-year-old neighbor grew up in the house. He watched with interest as Cuendet patched, sanded and wallpapered walls, rewired, added three bathrooms, carpeted, put in a new fence and sidewalks, and replaced 26 windows. Local craftspeople helped with everything from mouldings and sewing curtains to brochure design. Guests have use of a double parlor with a fire in the woodstove and a grand piano, the dining room, and lighted private tennis court with adjoining gazebo. Summer guests enjoy lemonade on the inn's wicker-filled porch.

Rooms and Rates: Five - Three with private baths. Examples: Jardin Room is former library, done in blues, queen bed, original clawfoot tub and pedestal sink - $79. Fur Elise overlooks river valley, has wood-burning stove, queen white iron bed, private bath with shower - $70. Fleur is attic room with sloping ceiling, double bed, has private balcony, shared bath - $64. Add tax.

Meals: Breakfast is served at 9 a.m. in the dining room or in parlor or to the guest rooms, and includes juice, tea or coffee on the porch, fruit such as baked apple with custard sauce; baked egg with havarti cheese, cinnamon French toast or cheese blintz, with cold fruit and hot muffins.

Dates open: Year 'round

Smoking: "Discouraged"

Children: No

Pets: No (but kennel nearby)

Other/Group Uses: Small business or group seminars midweek with lunch/dinner served. Weddings and reunions up to 40 people.

Nearby: Village of Marine, shops and ice cream parlor, 2 blocks. Marina and canoe rental, 1/2 mile. Bike trail Stillwater-Taylors Falls and x-c ski trail outside door. Sleigh rides. Adjacent to William O'Brien State Park.

Driving Time/Directions from Twin Cities: Within 1 hour. I-94 or Highway 36 to Stillwater, then Highway 95 to Marine on the St. Croix. Turn left on County Road 4, turn right on Fifth Street, follow signs.

Deposit: First night's lodging

Payment: Cash, personal or traveler's checks, VISA or MasterCard

Country Bed & Breakfast

32030 Ranch Trail
Shafer, MN 55074
612-257-4773

Owners/Operators:
Lois and Budd Barott

Country B&B is where Lois Barott shares memories of her childhood years growing up in the country with city folks who come to visit. There's a porch swing, fresh eggs from the chicken coop, and a big dog who loves to retrieve sticks. There's a country lane for walking. Birds sing and the atmosphere is peaceful and relaxing. This is how an imagined house in the country would be.

Lois Barott grew up with a brother and sister on these 60 country acres. Her parents had milk cows and they raised corn, oats, hay and soybeans. She and Budd raised their six children on the same property. For years, Budd commuted 138 miles a day to his job, and for some of those years, Lois joined him. She had a job soldering computer boards "when I got tired of milking the cows." After awhile, though, milking looked pretty good compared to that commute.

"I used to sit at work and think, 'There must be something else I can do,' " Lois said. After the last child left home, she quit her job and began toying with the idea of opening a B&B. Budd took early retirement and told her they ought to sell the house because it cost too much to heat for two people. Budd said that within a month, Lois had researched B&Bs and was determined to turn their home into one.

Their brick farmhouse was built in 1882 by Swedish immigrant Lars Thorsander. Renovation before opening the B&B included a new foundation, rewiring, reinsulating and reroofing, and adding trim and a deck in back. Three upstairs bedrooms became the guest rooms, a bath was added, and an attic became a sitting and reading room. Lois wallpapered and made comforters and cushions for the wicker furniture. The house is air-conditioned.

Rooms and Rates: All rooms have wicker furniture and handmade comforters and cushions, and the house is air conditioned. The Little Room ($47.70) has a double bed and shares a bath (new tub and shower) with the Lavender Room ($63.60), a large room that looks out over the front lawn and has a queen bed. The Green Room has a double bed and private bath with a clawfoot tub - $68.30. Rates are single or double and include tax.

Meals: Breakfast is served family style and includes ham, bacon or sausage, Budd's omelettes with fresh eggs, Lois' buttermilk pancakes with homemade maple syrup; fresh fruit; hashbrowns from scratch and sometimes homemade bread with homemade jams and jellies; Swedish egg coffee, tea, milk and juices. Guests can sit at the large kitchen table and talk while Barotts cook.

Dates open: Year 'round   **Smoking:** No

Children: 12 and older   **Pets:** No

Other/Group Uses: No

Nearby: St. Croix boat rides and canoeing in Taylors Falls, Wild River State Park (hiking, x-c skiing), 5 miles. Sunrise River tubing, 9 miles. Fishing, boating on Chisago area lakes, 3 miles. Snowmobile on Scandia Trail in Center City, 2 miles. Museums, pottery shops, flea markets, antique shops, restaurants.

Driving Time/Directions from Twin Cities: Within 1 hour. I-35 to Forest Lake Highway 8 exit, continue east through Center City to Shafer. Turn left on Co. Rd. 21 through town, continue past Co. Rd. 82, watch for Ranch Trail. Turn left, go about one mile. House is visible around the bend on the left.

Deposit: Full amount

Payment: Cash, personal or traveler's checks only   **51**

Historic Taylors Falls Jail

102 Government Rd.
Taylors Falls, MN 54084
612-465-3112

Owner/Operator:
Helen White

"Painter Beck, who got drunk Tuesday night, went to sleep on the front porch of Mrs. Guard's residence and woke up yesterday morning in jail." - Taylors Falls Journal, June 16, 1881.

These days, when people wake up in the Taylors Falls jail, they remember how they got there, and they got there on purpose.

The jail, well over 100 years old, has been restored by Helen White as a 16 x 24 foot bed and breakfast "home," with a small kitchen, loft bedroom, full bathroom and living room.

Listed on the National Register of Historic Places, the jail belongs to White as part of her property and house next door. What does one do with a jail in one's yard? "I had the building and knew I was going to restore it. There wasn't any good use for it except as a storage building, and that would've been a shame." Since it was the local lock-up, it has been a garage, a shoe repair shop, an ice house and a shop in which dog sleds were built.

"I was thinking about an apartment," she said, but "the architect said, 'What a pity more people can't enjoy it.' " White gutted the interior and started over, restoring the outside based on historic photos. The result was a B&B, which opened in 1981.

Guests are much more comfortable than those who first frequented one of the four cells. Two-by-fours have been installed as room dividers and ceilings to suggest the original cells, also made of 2 x 4s. Local artists and craftspeople have helped with everything from design to the iron steps and railings, the wood stove restoration and the pottery. It's heated with both wood and electricity.

Rooms and Rates: One loft double bed, and one sofabed. Bath has both tub and shower. $60 double. Weekends, two nights $120, third night free. Add tax. Extra person in room, $10; four-person maximum.

Meals: Breakfast fixings are in the refrigerator. Guests grind their own coffee and make juice, eggs, pancakes with local maple syrup, or have fruit, cereal, cheese, muffins or rolls.

Dates open: Year 'round   **Smoking:** Yes

Children: Yes, but limit is four people   **Pets:** No

Other/Group Uses: No

Nearby: Folsom House museum and Angels Hill Historic District, excursion boats, Interstate Park headquarters, shops and restaurants, 1-2 blocks. Two canoe rentals, 1 mile.

Driving Time/Directions from Twin Cities: Within 1 hour. I-35 to Taylors Falls/Highway 8; at bottom of hill, turn left, come up hill one block, turn left on Government Road. Jail is on right.

Deposit: Full amount

Payment: Cash, personal or traveler's checks only

Annandale

Thayer Hotel

Highway 55
Annandale, MN 55302
612-274-3371

Owners/Operators:
Wally Houle
Steve Houle, son

Many of the towns which were situated along the midwest's rail lines did not just spring up. Residents had to plead with and sometimes pay railroads to make a stop on their land, which would allow a town to survive.

In 1895, A.A. (Gus) Thayer did it the other way around -- the Soo Line Railroad actually paid *him* to build a hotel in Annandale, and gave him the land, besides. Thayer was manager of the Pleasant Lake Hotel across the street, but it burned down. The railroad found Annandale a key stop for prairie passengers' comfort, and wanted to promote resorting and fishing by Twin Citians. "Tourism was unheard of before that," said Wally Houle. "Soo Line advertised excursion fares for the weekend of $1.75 round trip." The hotel was "pretty classy" with its wild west balconies.

Houle didn't have it so good -- he had to buy the place. He was mayor of Annandale when the hotel was up for sale. The city wanted to preserve the structure, listed on the National Register of Historic Places, so, when no buyer was found, the city bought the hotel. Eight years and no buyer later, Houle decided to restore it himself.

For seven months, five carpenters plus other contractors worked more than full time for a May 1985 opening. "We took everything down to the bare walls, except in the lobby, where we worked around the tin walls and ceiling," Houle said. A total of 14 rooms now stand where 22 once did, all with original furniture or antiques and Victorian country decor.

Rooms and Rates: 14 - All with private bath with pull-chain toilets and clawfoot tubs; shared shower available. Queen beds in four, rest are doubles. Examples include: Room 202 has queen white iron bed, done in pink, white and green - $55. Room 201 has 1865 double bed with burled walnut headboard - $65. Bridal Suite with double wedding ring quilt on queen canopy bed - $75. Add tax. Midweek, corporate and single occupancy discounts.

Meals: Continental breakfast is included in the room rate on weekends, continental breakfast on weekdays. Lunch and dinner available in restaurant. Bar and lounge on premises.

Dates open: Year 'round   **Smoking:** Yes

Children: Yes (cots available)   **Pets:** Check with owners

Other/Group Uses: Meeting rooms for up to 20 people, small weddings.

Nearby: Minnesota Pioneer Park, 1.5 miles. City park with swimming, 6 blocks. Shopping, 2-4 blocks. Downhill and groomed x-c ski trails, 1 mile. Twenty five lakes within 5 miles.

Driving Time/Directions from Twin Cities: Within 1 hour. Highway 55 to Annandale, hotel is on the right side of the highway.

Deposit: $20

Payment: Cash, personal or traveler's checks, VISA or MasterCard

The Pratt-Taber Inn

706 W. Fourth
Red Wing, MN 55066
612-388-5945

Owners/Operators:
Jane Walker, Jan Molander,
Darrell Molander

When W.A. Pratt, one of Red Wing's first bankers, built a home in 1876, he spared no detail. Butternut woodwork with fancy fretwork was included, as was feather painting on slate fireplaces throughout the 13-room Italianate building. Yet the cost was $4,000. His daughter, a Taber by marriage, lived in the home until 1952, when it was made into apartments.

When the building later went up for sale, a realtor who was aware of the B&B movement contacted Jan and Darrell Molander and told them about the home's possibilities. Though they'd never stayed in a B&B, they went into a partnership and began work for an August opening. "Massive cleaning" and wallpapering, replumbing, rebuilding the foundation and porch, and removing a wall that plastered shut an opening to the dining room were among the necessary improvements to the home, listed on the National Register of Historic Places. Jan's sister, Jane Walker, is the live-in innkeeper.

Guests get a personal tour soon after check-in. One of the first things they learn is that there is coffee, lemonade, cider, cookies, donuts or pretzels always available in a bright kitchen with antique butler's cabinets. "I find that the kitchen is the thing that makes people feel most at home," Jan said. They also can use the sitting room, piano and library, provided the library is not rented as part of a three-room suite, which has a unique antique Murphy bed hidden in what appears to be a buffet.

Jane can explain the history of the antiques in each room. Look for attention to details, like an old-fashioned collar placed in a drawer or a Victorian woman's shoes on the floor.

Rooms and Rates: Six - Named for Pratt family members; plus the Library, which can sleep 8 in a 3-room suite for $179. Examples include: Henrietta's Room, double antique bed nearly nine feet high - $79. Aunt Aggie's Room, antique queen white iron bed, private sink - $69. Each two rooms share one full bath. Rates are double. Add tax. Midweek discounts.

Meals: Breakfast is served in the dining room or on the porch in the summer from 8:30 to 10 a.m. It may include homemade blueberry or apple coffee cakes, raisin bran or apple spice mini-muffins, sausage roll-ups, fresh fruit, juice, coffee, teas and hot chocolate. Snacks also available.

Dates open: Year 'round   **Smoking:** In parlor and sitting rooms

Children: "If quiet, well-behaved"   **Pets:** "Small, well-behaved"

Other/Group Uses: Murder mysteries, inn-to-inn biking or x-c skiing, reunions.

Nearby: Levee Park, downtown, riverboat and trolley car, 3 blocks. Trolley picks up guests at house in summer. Bikes furnished for a ride down Cannon Valley bike trail. Antiquing, golfing, skiing, pottery shopping.

Driving Time/Directions from Twin Cities: Within 1 hour. Highway 61 south to Red Wing. Turn right on Dakota, two blocks to Fourth. House is on right corner.

Deposit: First night's lodging

Payment: Cash, personal or traveler's checks, VISA or MasterCard

The St. James Hotel

406 Main St.
Red Wing, MN 55066
612-388-2846
Metro Line 227-1800

Owners:
Red Wing Shoe Company
Manager:
Gene Foster

In the 1870s, Red Wing claimed to be the largest wheat market in the world, shipping the golden grain down the river to hungry ports. Eleven businessmen built the first-class St. James Hotel in 1875, and it was heralded by newspapers and residents as an exceptional dining and lodging facility. It's now on the National Register of Historic Places.

As ownership changed, the Lillyblad family purchased the hotel and managed it for 72 years. Clara Lillyblad's cooking was reportedly so good that passenger trains made a special stop in Red Wing for a meal at "Clara's."

The hotel operated continuously until 1977, when the Red Wing Shoe Company purchased it and began extensive renovation to return it to its 1875 glory. Some original fixtures were discovered in the basement, the stairway was returned to its original place, and photographs of riverboats that docked in Red Wing became the source of names for the rooms.

"As with most older hotels, it had undergone so many furniture changes there really was not much that was useable," said Kathy Johnson, marketing manager. Antiques were hunted up, quilts were sewn for the beds, and each of the 41 rooms was designed individually.

When the shoe company re-opened the hotel again in 1979, it sported a shopping mall, a parking ramp, meeting and banquet rooms and three cafes and dining rooms. Another section was added in 1981 for 19 more rooms, though these rooms are as reminiscent of the late 1800s as the others.

This is a full-service hotel with luggage handling, elevators and turndown service. Guests receive complimentary champagne or Catawba juice on arrival and coffee, tea or hot chocolate in the morning, plus weekday paper.

Rooms and Rates: 60 - Each with its own decor and private bath, usually with writing tables. Expect brass, white iron or antique wood beds, and early American wallpaper, handmade quilts and carpet. About half have river view; 57 have both tub and shower. $60.50, $78.50, $95.50 (single whirlpools) or $115 (double whirlpools), single or double. Most rooms are $78.50 with queen beds. Add tax.

Meals: Three meals a day available in ground floor dining rooms and cafe, special Sunday brunch.

Dates open: Year 'round   **Smoking:** 7 non-smoking rooms

Children: Yes (18 and under free in room)   **Pets:** No

Other/Group Uses: Meeting and banquet rooms.

Nearby: Levee Park (riverboat and cable car depart from park in summer), 1 block. Sheldon Memorial Auditorium, 2 blocks. YMCA, 1/2 block.

Driving Time/Directions from Twin Cities: Within 1 hour. Highway 61 south to Red Wing. Hotel is on left side of Main Street (Highway 61 in town); turn left at stoplight by hotel to parking lot.

Deposit: First night's lodging or confirmation by credit card

Payment: Cash, personal or traveler's checks, VISA, MasterCard, AMEX, Discover, Diners Club or Carte Blanche

Quill & Quilt

615 W. Hoffman St.
Cannon Falls, MN 55009
507-263-5507

Owners/Operators:
Denise Anderson and
David Karpinski

Chalk "Quilt" up to Denise. Each bedroom in this 1897 Colonial Revival home has a handmade quilt courtesy of Denise, who quilts for relaxation. The "Quill" comes from her husband, who writes and works in public relations.

The two never thought their respective talents and hobbies would come into play in 1987 in a B&B in Cannon Falls. "Both of us were job-hunting several years ago and I read something about someone who had done a country inn," said Denise. "We thought, maybe a couple years away in Maine. But the house became available and we thought we could learn it on a small scale."

Still, they didn't rush into it, having visited more than 40 B&Bs in the U.S. and England over five years, making notes about innkeeping and comfort. Then, after the house was purchased and as wallpaper was being hung, David's PR department was eliminated in a corporate merger. Denise had quit as vice president of a metro area chamber of commerce to run the inn, so both were out of work.

But times are better. David is employed, the Cannon Falls bike/hike/x-c ski trail is drawing people, and their innkeeping is well-thought-of. The house, built by Dr. Alonzo T. Conley, a prominent physician from a family of area doctors and dentists, was in excellent shape. Even the third floor bee hives, so thick that heat from the fireplace melted honey that dripped down the chimney, had been removed.

Guests are treated to a tea and wine social about 6 p.m., with hot hors d'oeurves in the winter. They are welcome to use the porches, the unsticky fireplace in parlor, the deck out back, and the VCR or exercycle in the rec room.

Rooms and Rates: Four - All with private baths. Quilter's Room is on first floor, the former doctor's office; brass double bed, log cabin quilt, private bath down hall with tub and shower - $55. Upstairs: Colvill Suite has an king oak bed with canopy, brass and iron daybed in sitting room, done in blues and rust. Bath with double whirlpool, porch that looks out over river and ballfield - $95. Tracy's Room has queen brass and iron bed, window seat, done in rose and blues; bath down the hall with clawfoot tub and shower - $60. Grandmother's Fan - has patterned quilt by that name on double four-poster bed, done in red, cream and blue, stenciled, bath with shower only - $60. Add tax. Midweek and business discounts.

Meals: Breakfast is served in the dining room at 9 a.m. or by other arrangements and includes homemade muffins, fruit cup, juice, milk, fresh-ground coffee, bacon or sausage, and an entree, such as quiche, special egg dishes, ham and asparagus popovers or French toast. Picnics and evening meals by special arrangement.

Dates open: Year 'round

Smoking: Designated areas only

Children: 12 and older

Pets: No (dog on premises)

Other/Group Uses: Inn-to-inn biking, small weddings and retreats, dinners for groups. Dining room seats up to 10.

Nearby: X-c skiing, biking and hiking on Cannon Valley Trail, end of block. Cannon River tubing and canoeing rental pick-up, 3 blocks. Tennis courts, pool, park with swans, a few blocks. Golf course, swimming beach and boating, 3 miles. Downhill skiing, 15 miles. Antiquing, shopping, sightseeing.

Driving Time/Directions from Twin Cities: Within 1 hour. Highway 52 south to Cannon Falls exit. Left at top of exit (Highway 19) about 1/2 mile to 7th St. Left two blocks to Hoffman, turn right. House is on the right.

Deposit: First night's lodging

Payment: Cash, personal or traveler's checks, VISA or MasterCard

61

The Archer House

212 Division St.
Northfield, MN 55057
507-645-5661
Minn. toll-free 1-800-247-2235

Owner/Operator:
  Dallas Haas
General Manager:
  Mary Lethbridge

Described in the local press as "an episode of the grandest proportion in Northfield's history," the opening of the 50-room Archer House in 1877 drew three brass bands, as well as the local band. Today, the French Second Empire brick hotel on the Cannon River still draws out-of-towners.

In the years between, the hotel traded hands at least 31 times. It was known as the Manawa, Hotel Ball and the Stuart Hotel, but it always operated as a hotel. Haas restored the original name when he bought it in 1981.

And Haas has done more than restore a name. Originally, he renovated a small mall on one side of the hotel and had no interest in the hotel itself. But the mall generated business which used the hotel's parking lot and property, prompting the suggestion than Haas simply buy the hotel, too.

After he agreed, "reality set in," he said. Not only did he get a 30-room hotel with only 20 rooms operational, but the Jefferson Bus office and retail space were included in the deal. "Basically, nothing had been done to the rooms since the '50s," said Manager Mary Lethbridge, herself a former owner. A massive renovation was in order.

Downstairs, a tavern and restaurant serve three meals a day. A deli and retail shops are open on the ground floor. Only two rooms have been lost in the changes on the second and third floors. All decor is "country," with handmade quilts and decorations. Meeting rooms have been added. Guests in suites receive complimentary wine or champagne and handpainted, personalized wine glasses.

Rooms and Rates: 38 rooms and suites - Each has its own design and name. All double or queen beds. All have baths, some shower or tub only, some with bathroom partially enclosed in room. Stuart Room has pattern of old hotel in quilt, hand stencils on wall, shower only - $45. Bridal Suite has four poster bed, double wedding ring quilt on queen bed, double whirlpool - $110. Anniversary Suite has round double whirlpool, queen white iron bed - $120. Several other suites available. Rooms $40-50. Suites $90-$135. Add tax. Midweek discount.

Meals: Guests receive morning coffee and newspaper. Deli and restaurant on premises.

Dates open: Year 'round   **Smoking:** Yes

Children: Yes - no extra charge   **Pets:** No

Other/Group Uses: Banquet rooms for up to 200 people.

Nearby: Downtown shops and restaurants. Cannon River waterfall, Northfield Historical Society Museum (former bank where Jesse James gang was shot), historic tours, Northfield Arts Guild productions, 2 blocks. Hiking, x-c skiing, Carleton and St. Olaf college activities, 5-10 minutes.

Driving Time/Directions from Twin Cities: Within 1 hour. I-35 south about 35 miles to Highway 19 East. Continue to Division Street, turn left on Division. Hotel on left.

Deposit: First night's lodging

Payment: Cash, personal or traveler's checks, VISA, MasterCard or AMEX

Schumacher's New Prague Hotel

212 W. Main St.   Owners/Operators:
New Prague, MN 56071   John and Kathleen Schumacher
612-758-2133
Metro Line 445-7285

When John Schumacher, an executive chef with Marriott Hotel Corp., was transferred to the Twin Cities in 1974, he soon realized a lifelong ambition. "I discovered a sleeping beauty and found my chance to achieve the all-American dream -- owning my own business," he said. He found the New Prague Hotel, a small hotel designed by Cass Gilbert, the architect of the state Capitol.

The 1898 building was in a state of disrepair and had been for sale for more than five years. "I offered the owner $3,000 down on a contract for deed and she accepted." Schumacher left Marriott and devoted all his energies to creating this restaurant, capitalizing on his German heritage and the Czechoslovakian heritage of New Prague.

The hotel originally served traveling salesmen who used the nearby railroad for transportation. "When I bought the hotel, rooms rented for $2.50-$12.50 per night and showers could be taken for $1 in what is now the sitting room," he said. Schumacher remodeled, creating guest rooms furnished with Bavarian folk-painted furniture, and down comforters, linens and lighting from Europe. A complimentary bottle of German wine and custom-made chocolates await guests.

The media soon discovered the hotel, and articles and television spots contributed to its widening repution. The hotel is well known for its central European cuisine and unique atmosphere. Another major remodeling project recently included enlarging guest rooms and adding several fireplaces and double whirlpools, adding a gift shop with central European imports, and renovating two dining rooms. Schumacher and Kathleen, his wife, actively run the business and frequently visit with guests.

Rooms and Rates: 11, named after months (plus a guest cottage under construction) - $85, $120 or $135 weekends, $68, $95 or $110 weekdays. All upstairs, all with private baths, eight with double whirlpools, seven with fireplaces. Examples include the March Room, with queen bed with white eyelet canopy, German lace curtains, Czech chandeliers, fireplace and double whirlpool - $135 weekends, $110 weekdays. Add tax.

Meals: Three meals available in three dining rooms; Big Cally's Bavarian Bar also on ground floor.

Dates open: Year 'round   **Smoking:** Yes (no pipes or cigars)

Children: Yes, but discouraged   **Pets:** No

Other/Group Uses: Small business meetings, groom's dinners, reunions.

Nearby: Eighteen-hole golf course, x-c skiing, tennis in town. Canoe Minnesota River, 9 miles.

Driving Time/Directions from Twin Cities: Within 1 hour. I-35W to Highway 101/169 to Jordan, Highway 21 to New Prague. Or I-35 south to Highway 13 south to Highway 19 West to downtown New Prague.

Deposit: Full amount

Payment: Cash, personal or traveler's checks, VISA, MasterCard, AMEX or Discover

The Cosgrove

228 S. Second St.   Owner/Operator:
LeSueur, MN 56058   Pam Quist
612-665-2763

Carson Cosgrove had this house built as his own in 1893, when he was a hardware store owner dealing in farm machinery. He and other businessmen decided what LeSueur, a farming town located in the fertile Minnesota River Valley, really needed at the time was a sweet corn packing plant, so he became one of the founders of the Minnesota Valley Canning Co.

Later, one of that company's research biologists developed a sweet pea bigger even than the LeSueur pea, and it was named "Green Giant." Today, the company Cosgrove founded is named after that pea.

As the fifth owner, Pam Quist purchased the National Register home in July 1988 as a B&B inn that had been operating for three years.

"LeSueur is my home town," she said. "I grew up in a house one block down the alley from The Cosgrove." As a teenager, she babysat in the house, which was then a duplex.

Quist became interested in returning to LeSueur after attending a high school reunion. A friend still living in town called her to tell her when the B&B went up for sale.

Today, the house still has its original woodwork and the walls are loaded with paintings and prints. About 5 p.m., guests gather in the dining room for wine. Guests find a late-night snack inside their rooms, perhaps fresh grapes, carrot cake and amaretto.

Guests may use a sunporch in back of the house, dining and living rooms and front porch.

Rooms and Rates: Four - Three of which are rented at once because of shared bath, with tub and shower. Meg's Room has a porch which can be reached by climbing out the window/door, double bed. Rob's Room is done in red, white and blue theme, iron bed, fireplace. Amy's Room is octagonal, has lace parasol canopy over bed, done in yellows. Bradford's Room has fireplace, queen bed, done in green and peach. All rooms $65. Add tax.

Meals: Breakfast is served in the dining room at 9:30 a.m. "or by group consensus." Breakfast may include any combination of the following: Puffy Omelette with cheese sauce, Belgian waffles with strawberries and whipped cream, breakfast meats, fresh-squeezed juice and fruit, homemade breads, muffins or pastries.

Dates open: Year 'round except holidays   **Smoking:** In designated areas

Children: No   **Pets:** No

Other/Group Uses: No

Nearby: X-c skiing, golf, 2-3 miles. Antique shopping, in 20 mile area. Sakatah bike trail, 25 miles.

Driving Time/Directions from Twin Cities: Within 1 hour. I-494 south to Highway 169 southwest to LeSueur; take second exit to downtown. Second Street is one block up from Main Street.

Deposit: $25

Payment: Cash, personal or traveler's checks only

The Hutchinson House

305 NW Second St.
Faribault, MN 55021
507-332-7519

Owner/Operator:
Marilyn Vare Coughlin

Marilyn Vare Coughlin knew she wanted to be an innkeeper, but she wasn't going to enter into the profession lightly. It took two-and-a-half years and the work of seven realtors to find the "perfect" house and location.

She found the Hutchinson House while traveling for Federal Express, "but I never thought this particular house would become available." Later, while narrowing the inn search, a local realtor knew otherwise, and she bought it in May 1986. It fit her criteria for location, grandeur, historic importance and other factors.

The 1892 Queen Anne mansion was built by John Hutchinson, a furniture maker, mill owner and mortician who also was a one-term state legislator and served in the volunteer infantry during the Sioux Uprising. The Hutchinson family owned the home as a single-family dwelling until 1915, after which two apartments were added and major restoration work was done. Coughlin is the fourth owner of the 22-room mansion, listed on the National Register of Historic Places.

Innkeeping is a third career for her, following years as an art teacher and much success in sales for Xerox and Federal Express. It was a career goal to be a self-employed innkeeper. She designed and added two rooms and painted a 19.5-foot mural of cherubs on a wall in the suite, then opened in May 1987. The house is decorated with oriental rugs, unique light fixtures and antiques and Norwegian artifacts she has collected for many years.

Guests may use the Victrola and the collection of early 1900s records. Two parlors, a TV room and a large porch are open to guests. Beverages and hors d'oeurves are served in the late afternoon, and breakfast is always three courses.

Rooms and Rates: Five - All with window air conditioners and fans, hand-crocheted lace spreads and down comforters. Examples include the Violin Room, with a handmade violin in case, ceiling and two walls of wainscotting, balloon curtains, done in light mint green and peach, bath with shower only. Upstairs, Country Room has queen bed built-in under sloping roof, stereo system, bath with shower only; adjoining room sleeps two ($35 single, $50 double). Rates $50 single, $65 double. Hutchinson Suite has cherub mural, double walnut East Lake bed, stereo system, separate kitchen with refrigerator stocked with juices, perrier, champagne and chocolates - $85. Add tax. Midweek, senior, corporate discounts.

68

Meals: Breakfast is served in the front parlor, on the porch or to the guest rooms at a time arranged the night before. It may include homemade scones and muffins, bacon-wild rice quiche, whole wheat buttermilk banana crepes, fresh fruit, juices, coffee and tea.

Dates open: Year 'round   **Smoking:** On porch only

Children: Talk with innkeeper   **Pets:** No

Other/Group Uses: Inn-to-inn biking, small weddings, luncheons, catered dinners, tours, special events.

Nearby: Downtown shops and restaurants, 3 blocks. Treasure Cave Blue Cheese store, 4 blocks. Faribo woolen mills and outlet store, Sakahta Singing Hills Trail (biking, hiking, x-c skiing), nature center, 2 miles. Golf, parks, art studio.

Driving Time/Directions from Twin Cities: Within 1 hour. I-35 south to Faribault, exit to downtown. East to Third Avenue, turn right (south) 2 blocks.

Deposit: Half of room rate

Payment: Cash, personal or traveler's checks only

Northrop House

358 E. Main St.
Owatonna, MN 55060
507-451-4040

Owners/Operators:
The Northrop Family
Innkeeper: Richard Winston Northrop

This house was built before the turn of the century by H.M. Hastings for his daughter's wedding present. But it's best known in the area for its second and current owners, the Northrop family.

Dr. Harson A. Northrop purchased the home in 1943 as a birthday present for Tessie, his wife. Northrop was an osteopath-general practitioner who campaigned as a Republican candidate for governor, U.S. Senator and mayor.

The eight children raised there still own the home. The house had been maintained so Tessie could continue to live there. After she died in 1985, one of the siblings suggested turning the house into a B&B, though the others had not heard of the concept.

Their B&B opened in late 1987. The three guest rooms are named after well-known Northrops. A cousin of Harson Northrop was Cyrus Atwood Northrop, the second president of the University of Minnesota, for whom Northrop Auditorium is named. Another cousin was Filmore S.C. Northrop, a Yale philosophy professor who authored "The Meeting of East and West: An Inquiry into Human Understanding." And John Howard Northrop won the Nobel Prize and was with the Rockefeller Institute for Medical Research.

Richard, the only child of the eight living in Minnesota, is acting innkeeper. Guests have use of the dining room and two parlors downstairs, which include a fireplace, library and grand piano.

Rooms and Rates: Three - All upstairs facing the street, sharing bath with clawfoot tub and shower. Cyrus Atwood Northrop Room has a double white iron bed, brass chandelier, blue carpet and is done in blue and white. FSC Northrop Room has a double iron bed, gas/electric light fixtures, gold carpet, is done in yellow. John Howard Northrop Room has an double antique iron bed, hot pink carpet and beige and rose wallpaper. $44 single, $49 double. Add tax.

Meals: Breakfast is a buffet in the dining room served at a time arranged the night before and it may include fresh fruit, muffins, coffee, tea, hot chocolate and juices.

Dates open: Year 'round   **Smoking:** No

Children: Yes   **Pets:** No

Other/Group Uses: Wedding parties, private meals, catering available.

Nearby: Three golf courses, about 2 miles. Downtown shops, restaurants, Sullivan Bank tours, 4 blocks. Kaplan Woods and Parkway x-c skiing, walking and biking trails, 8 blocks.

Driving Time/Directions from Twin Cities: Within 1 hour. From I-35, take Bridge Street exit through downtown Owatonna. House is located on the east side of town near the Federated Insurance Company. Map sent.

Deposit: Confirmation by credit card

Payment: Cash, personal or traveler's checks, VISA or MasterCard

The Tudor on Bridge

473 W. Bridge St.
P.O. Box 664
Owatonna, MN 55060
507-451-8567

Owners/Operators:
Judy and Marlin Scholljegerdes

This landmark English Tudor home was built by Frank A. Seykora, an Owatonna businessman involved with what long-time Owatonna residents remember as the old Kelly Co., a mercantile store.

The house was started in 1918 and finished in 1921, only a half-mile or so from downtown but out in the country then. The land originally was sold by the U.S. government to Nelson Morehouse in 1857, and President James Buchanan signed the abstract releasing the property.

Seykora was not the only person fascinated by the English Tudor design. Marlin Scholljegerdes bought the home about 12 years ago. "He bought the house because he walked by it as a kid going to catechism" and always liked it, said Judy.

They didn't consider opening a B&B until more recently. Marlin had been a railroad depot agent, telegraph operator and dispatcher for 14 years, and he and Judy have been self-employed for 20 years.

"We have a house that people just love to come to -- they always have," Judy said. "If we make a go of it, we might look at innkeeping for our later years."

The first floor has beamed ceilings and a fireplace in the living room. Guests may play Judy's white grand piano. Furnishings are East Lake and Victorian antiques and there are lamps imported from England.

Now set on 1.5 acres, the garden is open for weddings. Judy also hosts special events with catering and a pianist at the piano.

Rooms and Rates: Three - All upstairs sharing bath with tub only. Blue Room has high carved walnut double bed, hand-crocheted bedspread, blue carpet, wood paneling - $46. Rose Room has wood floors with oriental rugs, maple bedroom set, double bed, rose and cream wallpaper - $46 double. Single $42. Celebration Room has high burled walnut carved double bed, marble-topped dressers, Tiffany-style lamp - $58. Add tax.

Meals: Breakfast is served in the dining room at 8 a.m. or at a time arranged the night before. It includes fresh fruit, juices, gourmet coffees, hot cereal and gourmet English muffins or hot breads.

Dates open: Year 'round   **Smoking:** No

Children: Talk with innkeepers   **Pets:** No

Other/Group Uses: Small meetings, seminars, garden weddings, luncheons and other special events.

Nearby: Owatonna Arts Center, 1 block. Kaplan Woods and Parkway x-c skiing, walking and biking trails, 2 blocks. West Hills pool and tennis complex, 1/4 mile. Downtown shops, Sullivan Bank tours, 1/2 mile.

Driving Time/Directions from Twin Cities: Within 1 hour. From I-35 south, take Bridge St. exit east past State Avenue. House is on right.

Deposit: Not necessary

Payment: Cash, personal or traveler's checks only

The Governor's House

P.O. Box 252
Askov, MN 55704
612-838-3296 or 612-838-3593

Owner/Operator:
Deloris Nielsen and friends

Around these parts, Governor Hjalmer Petersen is often remembered for his firey editorials in the Askov American newspaper and leading the community band from the bandstand in the village park next door to his house.

Hjalmer purchased the modest three-bedroom home in 1918, a year after it was built, and spent most of his adult life there, except when he needed to live in St. Paul. But as Josephine Krogh, a long-time Askov resident who knew the Petersens, would say, "He was one of the elite" -- not in terms of finances, but in terms of political prestige.

Petersen, elected as lieutenant governor, served as governor for only six months in 1936 after the death of Gov. Floyd B. Olson. Petersen also was a state representative, the Railroad and Warehouse Commissioner, and active in the formation of the Democratic Farmer-Labor party. Those editorials in the paper he and his brother founded were the beginning of an important career in state politics.

In 1986, Deloris Nielsen started a B&B in the home, sold by Petersen's widow. Nielsen had a vision for the home, wanting to provide needed overnight accommodations in Askov while educating travelers about Petersen and Askov, which was settled by Danish immigrants and still celebrates "Danish Days."

Nielsen and her mother, Della Jackson, did much of necessary restoration, including repairing walls and ceilings, painting, hanging new wallpaper and having new plumbing installed. Like Petersen himself, Nielsen spends a lot of time in the Twin Cities, where she works for Ramsey County. She comes up on weekends. Krogh, Christine Johansen or other friends in town run it when Nielsen can't. They serve a Danish breakfast and eventually Nielsen wants to dress in Danish style, too.

Guests have use of the entire house, including Hjalmer's piano in the dining room. They may read about Petersen in a 1987 book written by Steven Keillor, brother of another famous Minnesotan, Garrison Keillor.

Rooms and Rates: Three - All upstairs with queen-sized beds, wood plank floors. All share bath upstairs with tub only. Shower available in bath downstairs. White Room has yellow, green and white wallpaper. Blue room has a white iron bed and wicker dresser. Pink Room is the bright master bedroom, done in pink and white. $35, single or double. Add tax.

Meals: Breakfast is served in the dining room at a time arranged the night before and may include Danish Aebelskiver (ball pancakes) with jams and syrups, sausage, coffee, tea, milk and juice.

Dates open: Year 'round   **Smoking:** "Discouraged"

Children: Yes   **Pets:** No (local vet clinic will board)

Other/Group Uses: No

Nearby: Banning State Park (hiking, x-c skiing, snowmobiling, picnicking along Kettle River), 3 miles. Fishing, swimming at area lakes. Village park next door. Duluth, 1 hour away.

Driving Time/Directions from Twin Cities: Within 2 hours. I-35 north to East Highway 23/Askov exit. In town, turn right on first road (sign says GovernorsEj) to cross railroad tracks. House is on the left next to the village park.

Deposit: Not necessary

Payment: Cash, personal or travelers checks only

Palmer House Hotel

500 Sinclair Lewis Ave.
(at Main Street, of course)
Sauk Centre, MN 56378
612-352-3431

Owners/Operators:
Al Tingley and
Richard Schwartz

The Palmer House Hotel was built in 1901, a year before Sinclair Lewis was hired there. As the story goes, co-owner Al Tingley says, the young author-to-be spent a lot of time daydreaming and reading on the job. He finally was fired after he forgot to awaken a guest in time to catch a train.

The hotel is on the National Register of Historic Places and has reappeared in three books - as the Minniemashie House in "Main Street," as the American House in "Work of Art," and in "Corner on Main Street," the true story of innkeepers on Sinclair Lewis Avenue, which Tingley wrote.

Tingley is upfront about guests not getting "country" wallpapers with grapevine wreaths on the wall. "We wanted to keep the place as much like the original hotel as we could," and that includes baths down the hall. He and Schwartz have redone 25 of the 37 rooms, little by little, in what has not been an easy or cheap job. When they bought the hotel in 1974, it was in much worse condition than they expected, with major repairs and upgrading necessary, such as hoisting the building four inches to put in new footings.

The red oak lobby is the same as Lewis saw, as is the staircase. Twenty rooms have writing tables which Mr. Palmer himself bought for use by traveling salesmen. Light switches, however, could hardly be originals. "It was the first hotel outside Minneapolis to have running water and electricity," Tingley said. "The light switches were worn out in six months because people kept turning them on and off so much." Tingley and Schwartz have done most of the work themselves. Tingley is a gourmet cook and handles the restaurant business while Schwartz is the hotel man.

Rooms and Rates: 37 - All with sinks in rooms, furnished with antiques; three have private baths. Bath down hall for other rooms has original clawfoot tub. Also shower room. Rooms usually have a double bed. Rooms with bath down the hall - $19. Rooms with private bath - $25. Rooms with two twin beds, private bath - $35. Add tax.

Meals: Three meals available in restaurant. Dining room opens at 7 a.m.

Dates open: Year 'round   **Smoking:** In designated areas

Children: Yes   **Pets:** Yes

Other/Group Uses: No

Nearby: Sinclair Lewis' boyhood home, 3 blocks. Lake and park, 1 block. Theater, shopping, within 2 blocks.

Driving Time/Directions from Twin Cities: Within 2 hours. I-94 northwest to Sauk Centre exit, turn right and head downtown. Hotel is on left.

Deposit: $10

Payment: Cash, personal or traveler's checks only

Spicer Castle

P.O. Box 307
Spicer, MN 56288
612-796-5870

Owners/Operators:
Marti and Allen Latham
Innkeepers: Ginger and Renee Hanson

Spicer Castle is what might be called a B&B by popular demand.

The 1893 lakefront home, built as a summer home by the town's founder, has long been a local landmark, literally. Fishermen on the big lake used it as a landmark when finding fishing holes. But in 1987, Marti and Allen Latham started thinking seriously about turning the place into a B&B. "People coming through on tours would say, 'Oh, this should be a B&B,' " said Allen.

Built overlooking the lake, the home has an English tudor design with the interior warmth of a northwoods retreat. The main floor has two fireplaces, living and dining rooms and two porches, with original furnishings. Walls were covered with burlap about 1912. Upstairs, walls are wainscotting and floors are wood.

Allen Latham knows the history backwards and forwards -- he lived it. He is the grandson of John Spicer, who established Medayto Cottage and Farm two miles from town, accessible by the lake. Spicer experimented with new farming methods and machinery, and hired laid-off lumberjacks to clear land in the summers.

Allen spent his summers here. "My mother would never allow any changes. It was her childhood home and she didn't see any reason to change anything." Since the home had never been used consistently year 'round until it opened as a B&B in April 1988, some furnace and plumbing changes were necessary, but otherwise it's the same place Allen remembers running and jumping in, even riding bikes indoors "if the weather was bad enough." That's no longer encouraged in the National Register home, but guests are welcome to swim, canoe, or make friends with Dixie the horse out in back. Two guest cottages are available on the property, and more guest rooms may open. Tea is served to guests about 4:30 p.m.

Rooms and Rates: Four in main house - All with queen-sized antique beds, private baths with clawfoot tubs and showers. Agnes' Room is former maid's quarters, white iron bed, wainscotting on walls and ceiling - $60. Frances' Room is large room done in blues and greys - $80. Mason's Room has lake view, four-poster bed - $90. Jessie's Room has wainscotting, turret sitting area overlooking lake - $80. Add tax. Raymond's Cabin (log house, $80) and John's Lodge ($90) are private cottages; guests join B&B guests for tea and breakfast.

Meals: Breakfast is served by fireside in the dining room or on the porch overlooking the lake at 9 a.m. It may include Eggs Benedict or Belgian waffles, fresh fruit, juice, coffee, homemade muffins and cold cereals. Lunch and dinner available by advance arrangement, four person minimum.

Dates open: Weekends year 'round, daily in summer   **Pets:** No

Smoking: In designated area   **Children:** No

Other/Group Uses: Meetings, retreats, seminars, wedding receptions year 'round; catered lunches, dinners and buffets.

Nearby: Swimming, canoeing, visiting Dixie the horse on the five acres. Boat rentals nearby. Restaurants, antiques, craft shops, 2 miles or elsewhere in area. Sibley State Park (hiking, x-c skiing), 8 miles.

Driving Time/Directions from Twin Cities: Within 2 hours. Highway 12 west to Willmar, Highway 23 north to Spicer and east one mile on the south shore road of Green Lake. Map sent.

Deposit: One quarter of room rate or confirmation by credit card

Payment: Cash, personal or traveler's checks, VISA, MasterCard or AMEX

Evergreen Knoll Acres Country B&B

R.R. 1, Box 145   Owners/Operators:
Lake City, MN 55041   Bev and Paul Meyer
612-345-2257

You don't get family farms that are much more "family" than this.

Paul Meyer's grandparents settled on the farm "next door." His parents, Serenus and Helma Meyer, purchased 80 acres and built this farmhouse in 1919 after they married. They raised four children and a number of cows, chickens and hogs.

Since 1956, the farm has been Paul and Bev's. It's now 240 acres and has been specialized into a dairy-only operation, with about 65 Holsteins. Bev and Paul, too, have raised four children here.

"We used to call it a B&B years before it was because the relatives all came and stayed," jokes Bev. Officially, they redecorated and opened in October 1986, but the Meyers gradually grew into the hospitality industry. For years they had conducted tours of the farm for school groups. Paul's sister in Rochester, 35 miles from here, used to meet patients at the Mayo Clinic from as far away as Australia whom she'd invite out to experience a real, working Minnesota dairy farm.

As innkeepers of a farm B&B, Bev and Paul hoped to attract families with children who had never had the opportunity to see cows being milked. But it turns out it's not just kids who are interested. "You'd be surprised at how many older folks have never been on a farm," Paul said. Most guests, young or old, skip the 4:30 a.m. milking but will come out to the barn to watch the process at 4:30 p.m.

Bev offers coffee and a homemade dessert informally sometime before guests turn in for the night. The large family room has books, a TV and VCR and games, as well as a fireplace. Guests also can use the living and dining rooms downstairs, including the piano, and the deck outside. The house is air conditioned. A playpen and a rollaway cot are available for children at no extra charge.

Rooms and Rates: Three - All upstairs, sharing a new bath with shower only. Room 1 has a double white iron bed with an Amish quilt, done in beige. Room 2 has a double white iron bed and a separate sitting room with a wicker settee. Room 3 has two twin beds and some modern furniture. $35 single, $45 double. Add tax.

Meals: Breakfast is served in the dining room 8 to 9 a.m. or at an earlier time agreed upon by guests. It includes coffee, juice, fresh fruit, homemade bread, homemade cinnamon rolls or streusel coffeecake, herb-scrambled eggs and bacon or sausage, or French toast or pancakes.

Dates open: Year 'round   **Smoking:** Not in guest rooms

Children: Yes   **Pets:** Talk with innkeepers

Other/Group Uses: Group rental of entire house.

Nearby: Lake Pepin on the Mississippi in Lake City (marina, paddlewheel cruises), antiquing, restaurants, 8.5 miles. Downhill skiing, 12 miles. X-c skiing, birding and hiking in Frontenac State Park, 12 miles. Rochester, 35 miles.

Driving Time/Directions from Twin Cities: Within 2 hours. South on Highway 61 to Lake City. Turn right on Highway 63 south, go 3.5 miles to Wabasha County 15. Turn right, go 5 miles. Farm is on right.

Deposit: $20

Payment: Cash, personal or traveler's checks only

The Rahilly House

304 S. Oak St.
Lake City, MN 55041
612-345-4664

Owners/Operators:
Dorene and Gary Fechtmeyer

The vacant classic Greek Revival home, listed on the National Register of Historic Places, was purchased in 1983 by Dorene and Gary Fechtmeyer. Having had two fires and badly in need of repair, the huge home required new plumbing, wiring and roofing. A commercial kitchen was installed, and, after major redecorating, the B&B opened in June 1984.

The house had quite a life before falling into disrepair. John Stout built this house in 1862 for his sister, Eliza, and her husband, Harvey Williamson, Lake City's first postmaster. Since then, owners included Morris Russell, Lake City's first newspaper publisher; in 1883, Melissa Buck and her daughter, of the town's first clothing store; in 1901, Patrick Rahilly, state senator and Irish immigrant; in 1932, Rahilly's son-in-law, McCahill; in 1963, George Enz, Ziegfeld Follies singer.

Guests can look at a photo album showing the stages of restoration. Guests have use of the screened porch, upstairs sundeck, parlor, dining room and living room, which can also be transformed into a guest room. An antique Victrola can be played. A social hour with hors d'oeuvres is at 5:30 after 5 p.m. check-in. The quilts and antiques are for sale.

Rooms and Rates: Seven - Each with a double bed; one with private bath, other six share three baths. Three rooms have in-room sinks and three have fireplaces. Examples include: Doughty Room, used to be the dining room and has original antique buffet and window seats, beveled glass - $80. Williamson Room has pocket doors which can be pulled shut and two double beds; a huge bath off the dining room is used - $60 double. Other rooms are upstairs and examples include: Russell Room with a working fireplace, sleigh bed, done in beiges - $70. Buck Room, also in beiges, has antique brass bed - $60. Rahilly Room has cannonball four-poster bed, white marble fireplace, is done in dark green and rose, has a sink - $80. Rates are double. Add tax.

Meals: Breakfast is served family-style in the dining room at 9 a.m. and includes freshly-ground coffee (served early), juice, homemade muffins, pastries or breads, fresh fruit in season, plus a varied entree, such as seafood quiche or Tahitian French Toast.

Dates open: Year 'round   **Smoking:** In designated areas

Children: 12 and older   **Pets:** No

Other/Group Uses: Small business groups, murder mysteries, group meals.

Nearby: Bikes for guests' use, hay rides, holiday special events. Lake Pepin on Mississppi in Lake City (marina, paddlewheel river cruises), downtown restaurants and shops, 2 blocks. Downhill skiing, 6 miles. X-c skiing, birding, hiking at Frontenac State Park, 5 miles.

Driving Time/Directions from Twin Cities: Within 2 hours. Highway 61 south to Lake City. Turn right on Marion Street, go two blocks. House is on corner of Oak and Marion.

Deposit: First night's lodging

Payment: Cash, personal or traveler's checks only

Red Gables Inn

403 N. High St.
Lake City, MN 55041
612-345-2605

Owners/Operators:
Bonnie and Bill Saunders

"The most fun I've ever had" is how Bill Saunders describes innkeeping.

It's a good thing he and Bonnie like it, too. They gave up jobs in California, bought this 1865 home, sold their home, moved here and put in four solid months of work before opening.

And all that was done in order to slow down. Bill held a high-pressure job that involved extensive travel, one that a doctor told him he best give up. He and Bonnie, an OB-GYN nurse, lived outside L.A., and they considered moving to Minnesota to be near her sister in Rochester. "He'd always been teasing about a B&B," Bonnie said. "They always *thought* I was teasing, but I wasn't," Bill answered. "I'm a frustrated restauranteur with no formal experience."

They couldn't find a suitable home in Rochester, but they almost bought one in New York state. When Bonnie's sister heard that, she got busy with a realtor and they came up with this Victorian Lake City home.

It was built by William Bessey, a Wisconsin wheat merchant. It was later owned by Calvin Neal of the Neal-Johns Wagon Works, a local company that turned out 5,000 wagons a year. Since the 1940s, it changed hands several times. When Saunders found it, it needed new plumbing, rewiring, adding two new baths upstairs and sinks in guest rooms, plus stripping all the old wallpaper, sanding, painting, and putting new wallpaper up -- even on the ceilings in the guest rooms.

Guests are welcome to enjoy wine and hors d'oeuvres served at twilight in the parlor or on the screened porch. Saunders will pick up guests from the local marina. Bikes are available for guests' use.

Rooms and Rates: Four - All upstairs with ceiling fans. Cotton Blossom has a king white iron and brass bed, antique cherry wardroble, done in blue and white, pedestal sink, shares bath with clawfoot tub with shower - $58. Annie Laurie has a high Victorian walnut double bed with crocheted spread, maple wardrobe, done in rose and cream, pedestal sink, shares bath - $48. Nominee has queen white iron and brass bed, Victorian wardrobe, done in dark blue and white, bath with shower only - $68. Belle Lee has queen brass bed, mahogany wardrobe, done in rose and white, bath with shower only - $68. Add tax. Ask about winter ski packages.

Meals: Breakfast is served in the dining room or on the porch at 9 a.m. It is a buffet that includes juices, seasonal fruits, cheeses, homebaked breads and pastries, egg dishes with meat or meat as a side dish, coffee, tea and milk. Gourmet picnic baskets or evening summer barbeques are available by prior arrangement.

Dates open: Year 'round   **Smoking:** In designated areas

Children: Over 13   **Pets:** No (dogs on the premises)

Other/Group Uses: Small retreats, wedding receptions, reunions, gourmet suppers, lunches, brunches, clubs hosted for teas or dessert and coffee.

Nearby: Lake Pepin on the Mississippi at Lake City (marina, paddlewheel river cruises), 6 blocks. Downtown restaurants and shops, 3 blocks. Downhill skiing, 6 miles. X-c skiing, birding, hiking, Frontenac State Park, 5 miles.

Driving Time/Directions from Twin Cities: Within 2 hours. Highway 61 to Lake City. At West Doughty Street, turn right to High Street. Inn is on the corner.

Deposit: First night's lodging or confirmation by credit card

Payment: Cash, personal or traveler's checks, VISA or MasterCard

Lake City

The Victorian Bed & Breakfast

620 S. High St.
Lake City, MN 55041
612-345-2167

Owners/Operators:
Sandy and Joel Grettenberg

Sandy and Joel Grettenberg got more than apples one fall day in 1984 when they drove from Rochester to this Mississippi River town.

Lake City's orchards are well known, and making the 35 mile trip for apples was a pleasant outing. But they saw that this home overlooking the river's Lake Pepin was for sale, and they ventured to peak in the windows. "We got home and it's just kept gnawing at us," said Sandy. "Our daughters are looking at us like this is our mid-life crisis." With a Rochester home located just blocks from their jobs and almost paid off, they had no reason to buy another home. But they fell in love with the house, and buy it they did.

In 1986, after another daughter finished school, they opened the B&B. "We had stayed at some B&Bs outside New Orleans and out west," Sandy said, and they knew in 1984 they'd eventually be innkeepers. Joel still teaches third and fourth grades in Rochester and Sandy also commutes part-time to teach preschool. "We have the best of everything. We're still part of the Rochester community and the Twin Cities are close, too."

The home was built in 1896 by Juliette and Thomas Morrow. He was the director of a bank and owned several area farms. The architect designed their home so bay windows and other angles provide a lake view from every room.

No alterations to the home were made over the years, the original woodwork and stained glass windows remained, and Sandy and Joel's daughters were the first children to live in the house. The home had been well-maintained, and new carpet and wallpaper and adding a bathroom were all that was necessary before opening.

The home is furnished with antiques and family heirlooms, including antique music boxes. The parlor and its TV, the dining room, the living room and its piano and the front porch are open for guests' use.

Rooms and Rates: Three - All upstairs with handmade quilts and lake views. All share bath with large clawfoot tub only; bath downstairs available with shower. Kari's Room has a six-foot carved ash double bed - $45. Teresa's Room has two wicker twin beds or a king bed and a sitting room with view - $50. Juliette's Room has a queen bed with a sleeper sofa, oriental teak and cherry chests - $50. Add tax. Rates are double. Single $5 less. Extra person in room, $5.

Meals: Continental breakfast is served in the dining room, on the porches or to guest rooms before 9:30 a.m. It includes coffee, juice, muffins, biscuits and a fruit plate or cup.

Dates open: Year 'round

Smoking: On porches only

Children: Over 10

Pets: No

Other/Group Uses: No

Nearby: Lake Pepin on Mississppi in Lake City (marina, paddlewheel river cruises), 1 block. Downtown restaurants and shops, 3 blocks. Downhill skiing, 6 miles. X-c skiing, birding, hiking at Frontenac State Park, 5 miles.

Driving Time/Directions from Twin Cities: Within 2 hours. Highway 61 south to Lake City. Go through the stoplight five blocks to High Street and Lakewood Avenue. House is on the corner.

Deposit: First night's lodging

Payment: Cash, personal or traveler's checks only

The Anderson House

333 N. Main St.
Wabasha, MN 55981
612-565-4524   535 5467
Minn. toll-free 1-800-862-9702

Owners/Operators:
Jeanne Hall
John Hall, son

Listed on the National Register of Historic Places, this is Minnesota's oldest operating hotel. Service has never ceased since opening in 1856, and many of the original fixtures remain. So does the family ownership, now in its fourth generation. Grandma Anderson's cooking, learned in the Pennsylvania Dutch Amish country, remains a mainstay of the hotel.

The hotel has received national publicity for its "cat house" offer - guests can have a cat assigned to them during the stay, and it will be brought to their room sometime in the early evening for the overnight. The idea is a big hit with cat lovers who had to leave Puff home. Another service is a holdover from earlier days: order up some hot bricks for the foot of the bed.

Guest rooms are upstairs from two large dining rooms. Since the hotel is more than 130 years old, the squeaky floors, doors that don't shut exactly tight, hallway floors that aren't quite level, and baths down the hall seem appropriate. There are no elevators or bellboys, and there's no extra charge for television in the room.

Downstairs, an apartment has been redone into a 150-seat dining room. The room's Pennsylvania Dutch wallpaper emphasizes the traditions carried on in the kitchen. A sun porch and another dining room also are available. A bakery sells take-home treats and an ice cream parlor has sundaes and sandwiches.

Rooms and Rates: 42 - Rooms are done in bright and light blues, greens, pinks and reds; some original furniture remains. The Bridal Suite has green carpet; white, pink and green wallpaper; marble-top furniture and private bath. The Mayo Suite occupies the turret and is done in red and white. $29.50 - $59 singles or doubles, $71-$89 for suites, including one with whirlpool. Add tax. Packages available.

Meals: Three meals a day available in ground floor dining rooms, plus bakery and ice cream parlor. On Sunday, dinner only served 11:30 a.m. - 8 p.m; ice cream parlor open and serving sandwiches.

Dates open: Year 'round   **Smoking:** Yes

Children: Yes   **Pets:** Yes ("house cats" available)

Other/Group Uses: Meetings, bus tour lunches, groom's dinners, receptions.

Nearby: Downtown, 2 blocks. Mississippi River, 1 block. Country roads, gift and antique shops, fishing, boating.

Driving Time/Directions from Twin Cities: Within 2 hours. Highway 61 south to Wabasha, easy to find on Main Street.

Deposit: $25

Payment: Cash, personal or traveler's checks only

Eden B&B

R.R. 1, Box 215
Dodge Center, MN 55927
507-527-2311

Owner/Operator:
Margaret Chapin

When she was 15, Margaret Chapin moved to the farm across the street from this one. At 19, with a year of teacher training, she walked into a one-room school to teach 35 pupils in eight grades, which earned her $50 a month. At 23, she quit teaching and settled in to this home as a new bride. She had been the girl-next-door and married the son of the neighboring farm family.

Her late husband was one of five brothers who shared one bedroom upstairs. Lottie and T.W. Chapin bought the farm in 1907 and raised the five sons and one daughter here. At the turn of the century, "Eden was a flourishing little village that boasted two stores, a blacksmith shop, stock yards, a church, a post office and a cheese factory," said Margaret. When autombiles commonly were used, area residents bypassed Eden to patronize larger towns. By 1935 it was a ghost town, she said. Guests can see the parsonage and remains of the cheese factory and hike on an abandoned railroad bed.

After raising four children and being widowed, Margaret did a lot of traveling (including B&Bs in Germany). She decided that opening a B&B would add purpose and joy to her now-empty home. The buildings and the 290 acre-farm are rented out, and dairy cows are in the pasture next door. The home is among many trees; it was built in the middle of a sulky race track by a speculator from Mantorville.

The B&B opened in August 1986. There is some modern furniture and carpet plus family antiques and heirlooms. The dining room fireplace, the parlor and the family room with TV are open to guests.

Rooms and Rates: Four - All upstairs. The Green Room has light green carpet and walls, double bed. The Rose Room has a high carved double bed brought from England, pink, rose and blue wallpaper with an aquamarine carpet. They share a bathroom with a tub and shower - $30. The Blue Room has a matching black walnut bedroom set, blue velvet drapes and bedspread, done in blues, beige and yellow, private bath with shower only - $50. The Red and White Room has red brocade-like wallpaper, queen brass bed, red carpet and curtains, private bath with shower only - $50. Add tax. Rates are single or double.

Meals: Breakfast is served in the dining room at a time arranged the night before and includes coffee, fresh fruit or juice, homemade caramel rolls, muffins, and a main dish, such as hashed brown potato-egg hot dish or quiche.

Dates open: Year 'round

Smoking: "Discouraged"

Children: Yes

Pets: No

Other/Group Uses: No

Nearby: Four-mile hike on abandoned railroad bed. Mantorville, historic town with theater, antiquing, golf, restaurant, 6 miles. Rice Lake State Park (hiking, Indian Mounds), 9 miles. Rochester, 25 miles.

Driving Time/Directions from Twin Cities: Within 2 hours. I-35 south to Owatonna, Highway 14 east to Highway 56, turn left (north). Right (east) on County Road 16 about a half-mile. Inn is on the right.

Deposit: $10

Payment: Cash, personal or traveler's checks only

Canterbury Inn B&B

723 Second St. SW
Rochester, MN 55902
507-289-5553

Owners/Operators:
Mary Martin and
Jeffrey Van Sant

For Mary Martin and Jeffrey Van Sant, opening a B&B was more a question of where than when or how. The two women met in St. Louis and became good friends while getting divorced. Jeffrey was a church administrator and Mary was a nurse. "We both like to take care of people," Jeffrey said. "Besides, we had the same china pattern," she adds with a laugh.

One of the problems, though, was that most towns that depend on tourism in this part of the country have only seasonal lodgings. They checked into locations as far away as the Caribbean. On one trip to Rochester, they realized that people coming to the Mayo Clinic and IBM, for instance, would mean year 'round business. The Rochester realtor they called had been hoping someone would open a B&B there and had a property in mind.

The house for sale was used as a French restaurant, Broadstreet Cafe, that had outgrown the house. Dairyman Samuel Hall had built the home in 1890, and it remained in his family until the mid 1970s. The restaurant owners were the first owners outside the family. "Nobody ever chopped up the house or painted or did anything funny to it," Mary said. They bought it, put in new bathrooms and redecorated, then opened in April 1983.

Guests are treated to "tea" from 5:30 to 7 p.m. with wine and baked brie, pate or other hors d'oeuvres. They may use the living and dining rooms downstairs. Martin and Van Sant include special touches, like blanket covers on the beds and a willingness to drive guests to appointments or provide flexible breakfast times.

Rooms and Rates: Four - All have private bath with shower and tub, and are decorated with family period pieces and done with natural wood. Bed sizes in the four rooms are queen, king, two twins, and either a king or two twins. $55 single, $65 double. Add tax.

Meals: Breakfast is served any time in the dining room or guest rooms and it may include juices, homemade breads, Norwegian fruit soup, baked apples or fresh fruit and an entree such as Grand Marnier French toast, baked German apple pancakes, wild rice waffles, pesto omelettes or eggs benedict. ("Tea" may suffice as evening meal.)

Dates open: Year 'round

Smoking: First floor only

Children: "By consultation"

Pets: No

Other/Group Uses: No

Nearby: Mayo Clinic and St. Marys Hospital, 3 blocks. Antiques, restaurants, shops, theaters, symphony, jewelry and art galleries, 4-6 blocks. Mayowood, about 5 miles. X-c skiing, golf, 10 miles. Canoeing Zumbro River, 30 miles.

Driving Time/Directions from Twin Cities: Within 2 hours. Highway 52 south, exit on Second St. SW, turn left and about nine blocks.

Deposit: First night's lodging or confirmation by credit card

Payment: Cash, personal or traveler's checks, VISA or MasterCard

Lund's Guest House

500 Winona St. SE
Chatfield, MN 55923
507-867-4003

Owners/Operators:
Marion and Shelby Lund

Since 1973, Marion and Shelby Lund have lived in Oakenwald Terrace, a mansion on the National Register of Historic Places that they run as lodging for the elderly, and through which they often give tours. It's filled with many years' collecting of antiques, and they had even more that were stored away.

It wasn't unusual that when someone would get stranded overnight in Chatfield, where there's presently no motel or hotel, the Lunds would be asked to lodge the travelers in an extra bedroom.

So, it seemed natural that they enter the hospitality business and use some of their antiques and their home decorating and restoration knowledge as well. But instead of converting their own home, they decided on a guest house just up the street, where travelers can enjoy privacy. On a Sunday morning walk, Shelby found a 1920s home for sale just three blocks away. "We got inside and we really kind of liked it," he said. Originally, the single-family home was built as a wedding present by a father for his daughter, the bride.

In February 1987, electricians, carpenters and plumbers began work that snowballed beyond original plans, Lunds admit. The house ended up with new plumbing and wiring, as well as redecorating, with Marion papering and Shelby painting. Shelby traced down a circa 1930 electric stove he wanted to buy earlier at an auction and bought it from the new owner, and it's been installed back into the kitchen. By June 1987, the antiques were in place and the guest house opened.

Lawn croquet, checkers, an ironing board and laundry facilities in the basement, an electric organ and a living room fireplace are all in place for guests' use. A big screened front porch and small screened back porch are popular for return to life in the slow lane.

Rooms and Rates: Four - Downstairs, one bedroom has a double bed, is done in beiges, bath with clawfoot tub only. Second bedroom has a matching art deco maple bedroom set, gold bedspread, bath with shower only. Upstairs, one bedroom has a double bed with scrollwork on the wood bedroom set. $35 single or double. Second bedroom has two twin beds with carved headboards and satin spreads - $40 single or double. Half bath upstairs plus bathroom with both tub and shower. Add tax. Extra person in room, $5.

Meals: Rolls and juice are provided for breakfast, and the kitchen has a coffeemaker, microwave and electric stove and oven for guests' use.

Dates open: Year 'round

Smoking: On porches only

Children: Talk with owners

Pets: Talk with owners

Other/Group Uses: Whole house rental for families/reunions.

Nearby: Downtown park, canoe rental, restaurants, 4 blocks. International band music lending library, 6 blocks. Snowmobile trail, edge of town. Root River State Trail (biking, hiking, x-c skiing), 9 miles. Self-guided fall foliage tours in area available (ask innkeepers). Amish farms, tractor collection, art gallery.

Driving Time/Directions from Twin Cities: Within 2 hours. Highway 52 south to Chatfield. Turn east two blocks to Winona Street.

Deposit: Confirmation by credit card

Payment: Cash, personal or traveler's checks, VISA or MasterCard

The Ellery House

28 S. 21st Ave. E.
Duluth, MN 55812
218-724-7639

Owners/Operators:
Joan and Jim Halquist

Opening Duluth's second B&B in June 1988 was a career and personal move for Joan and Jim Halquist, who came to Duluth and bought this Queen Anne Victorian specifically to live in and run as a B&B.

"We love old houses and we love Duluth," Jim said. Joan has had relatives in Duluth, including a grandfather who practiced dentistry in West Duluth for 60 years. Jim had nearly seven years experience in the hospitality industry at Spring Hill Conference Center, and he believed his skills would be transferable to a B&B. They had restored historic homes and loved their homey "feel." Also, "Joan and I wanted to work together in a small business." They divide the cooking, cleaning and chores, and are able to be home with their three-and-a-half year old son.

Halquists found the home, with its turrets, balconies and leaded glass, after seeing just three others with a realtor. The name is from an early owner, Ellery Holliday, a Duluth real estate promoter. It was also owned by William Jeffrey, an auditor for Oliver iron mining company and Pittsburg Steamship Co., and Thomas Wahl, who was involved in constructing the St. Lawrence Seaway.

The most recent owners were a professional couple who had done quite a bit of restoration work. The home needed some renovating and decorating in order to open, which was accomplished in what the Halquists call two "whirlwind" months.

Guests are welcome to use the living room and parlor downstairs, including the grand piano, and they may talk Joan into accompanying them on her violin.

Rooms and Rates: Five - All upstairs and decorated with antiques. Ellery Suite is in rust and cream, queen brass bed, sitting room with daybed, balcony, private bath with tub only - $75. Lilla's Room ($60) is in blues and whites with double white iron bed, corner sink, shares bath with Daisy's Room and Sleeping Porch. Daisy's has queen bed, done in peach - $55. Sleeping Porch has double bed and is furnished in wicker - $60. Shared large bath has original marble shower stall, clawfoot tub, pedestal sink. Thomas Wahl Room has whirlpool under bay window, fireplace, double bed, private bath - $75. Add tax. Rates are double. Single $5 less. Corporate, midweek, group discounts.

Meals: Breakfast is served in the dining room from 8 to 9 a.m. and includes juice, milk, homemade scones or muffins and an entree du jour, such as oatmeal souffle, "Featherbed Eggs," omelettes or waffles.

Dates open: Year 'round   **Smoking:** No

Children: Under 12, talk with innkeepers   **Pets:** No (dog on premises)

Other/Group Uses: Reunions. Ask about package weekends.

Nearby: University of Minnesota-Duluth and College of St. Scholastica, 1 mile. downtown, 21 blocks. Lake Superior, 4 blocks. Highway 61/London Road (restaurants), 2 blocks.

Driving Time/Directions from Twin Cities: Within 3 hours. I-35 to Superior Street (Highway 23) exit. Follow Superior to 21st Avenue. Turn right; it's the second house from the corner on the east (left) side of 21st.

Deposit: $50 or confirmation by credit card

Payment: Cash, personal or traveler's checks, VISA or MasterCard

Fitger's Inn

600 E. Superior St.
Duluth, MN 55802
218-722-8826 (collect)
Minn. toll-free 1-800-223-2774,
    ext. 450

Owner/Operator:
    Fitger's Inn Limited Partnership
General Manager: Marvin Miller

Fitger's Inn opened in November 1984 in a serues of historic buildings, listed on the National Register of Historic Places. The 10-building complex had been constructed over the years as a brewery in downtown Duluth. When the last beer was bottled in 1972, Fitger Brewing Company, the last of a long list of brewery owners, closed its doors on Duluth's longest running business. When the buildings opened again, they were a 48-room hotel, restaurant, large shopping mall and parking lot overlooking Lake Superior.

Sidney Luce was the first to try brewing in Duluth,which he intended as an economic stimulant during an 1857 depression. In 1882, another owner hired German immigrant August Fitger, a German brew school graduate. Within two years, Fitger owned half the company.

Fitger beer was more in demand than ever as the Iron Range's miners thirsted. Prohibition didn't stop success - pop, "near beer" and cigars were sold. Just before World War II, 100,000 barrels of Fitger beer were produced a year.

The hotel itself has been built in the former bottling plant. The loading dock's beams can still be seen out the windows on the second level, lake side. The original teller's cage and safe are in the lobby; the hotel lobby was the shipping and receiving office. In many rooms, the massive exterior rock walls have been left uncovered. Visitors can take a self-guided walking tour of the complex. Parking ramp is free (it used to be the barn for beer wagon horses).

Rooms and Rates: 48 - All with tub and shower and queen or king-sized beds. Thick carpeting, antique reproductions and turn-of-the-century decor, perhaps with two or four-poster beds. Rates range from $73.95 for a single, street-side, to $260 for the Lake Superior Suite, a room the size of three regular rooms, with a four-poster bed and single whirlpool. Most rates in the $80-$90 range. Lakeside rooms $10 more. Suites also $135 and $160. Add tax. Packages and seasonal corporate rates.

Meals: Three meals available in Augustino's Italian Ristorante in the complex. Other restaurants open in the mall.

Dates open: Year 'round   **Smoking:** Yes

Children: Yes   **Pets:** No

Other/Group Uses: Small group room, banquet rooms, 160-seat theater.

Nearby: Shopping and dining in mall complex; outdoor patio by lake. Shops springing up along Superior Street; many shops within walking distance.

Driving Time/Directions from Twin Cities: Within 3 hours. I-35 to Duluth, follow Superior Street to Fitger's, on the right.

Deposit: First night's lodging or confirmation by credit card

Payment: Cash, traveler's checks, VISA, MasterCard, AMEX or Diners Club

The Mansion

3600 London Rd.
Duluth, MN 55804
218-724-0739

Owners/Operators:
Sue and Warren Monson and family

Nobody can say the Monsons haved named their B&B inaccurately. This is the spectacular estate of Harry Dudley, a mining engineer who did business internationally, and Marjorie Congdon Dudley, one of the six Congdon children born and raised at Glensheen mansion, just a half mile away.

Marjorie and Harry were married in 1918. In 1930, Harry brought her back to the neighborhood of her childhood, to live in a home that reportedly cost $100,000 at the time, excluding land and other buildings. The Dudleys raised two boys in the home, which had 13 bedrooms, 10 of which were for staff or guests.

In 1982, the Monsons found the mansion while looking for land on Lake Superior. "We fell in love with it and had to have a reason to swing it," said Sue Monson. The "reason" was a B&B she and three children would run in the summers while Warren, a doctor, would keep his practice in Browerville. As the first B&B in Duluth, its operation is allowed only six months a year by city officials.

Before opening in May 1983, the house needed to be completely furnished and outfitted. The next big projects were reinsulating, after getting a first-year utility bill as big as some people's mortgages, and replacing 75 missing storm windows out of 300 total. Warren has since moved his practice to West Duluth.

Guests may use the seven acres of grounds, 525 feet of shoreline, a huge screened porch, living room, dining room, gallery, library and first floor bathroom.

Rooms and Rates: 10 - Plus a three-bedroom apartment. All rooms have queen or king beds. Four are former servants' rooms, so they're smallest. The Houseman's Room has private bath, is on first floor - $95. The Yellow, Peach and Beige rooms share two baths - $75 each. Pink Room has antiques, a china tub - $105. Green and Blue rooms share interconnecting bathroom and face lake - $105 each. The South Guest Room is a huge lakeside room, also with china tub - $145. The Anniversary Suite is only room on the third floor, with lake view, private bath - $145. Add tax. Extra person (over 2) in room, $25. Two-night minimum required on weekends; remaining single nights sold one week ahead of that weekend.

Meals: Breakfast is from 8:30 - 9:30 a.m. in the dining room and includes five kinds of juice, various entrees such as French toast or egg dishes, breakfast meat, toast or muffins, danish, caramel rolls, turnovers or croissants.

Dates open: May 15-Oct. 15 and most winter weekends. Closed Wednesdays.

Children: Talk with innkeepers   **Smoking:** In library and porch

Pets: No   **Other/Group Uses:** No

Nearby: Glensheen Mansion, 1 block, 10 minutes to downtown Duluth.

Driving Time/Directions from Twin Cities: Within 3 hours. I-35 to Duluth, follow signs for Highway 61/North Shore Drive, look for 3600 signs on right past Glensheen.

Deposit: First night's lodging

Payment: Cash, personal or traveler's checks, VISA or MasterCard

Just Like Grandma's

113 W. Main St.
Osakis, MN 56306
612-859-4504

Owners/Operators:
Carol and Steve Mihalchick

For more than 70 years, this 1903 Queen Anne Victorian home in downtown Osakis was owned by the Brown brothers. The Browns owned and operated a mercantile store in town. They bought the house in 1910, after a series of owners, for their younger brothers and sisters.

It took Carol and Steve Mihalchick two days to decide to buy it from the Brown family. "My friend's parents live in town," said Carol, who came up for a visit in 1983. "My friend wanted to tour it" when it was offered for sale. Carol agreed to go and it was she who fell in love with it. "I brought my husband up and two days later we had our purchase offer in."

Carol, who runs boutiques in Minneapolis, wanted to turn the home into a summer business. "Everything but the woodwork" needed work. The floor was jacked up and the house was replastered, replumbed and redecorated. A carriage house on the property also has been restored. The main floor of the house and the carriage house now are known as the "Just Like Grandma's" gift shop, which offer country decorations and gifts.

The gift shop and guest rooms opened in 1984. Many customers were curious about the upstairs of the house and interested in a local B&B. "It's been popular with overnighters who are in town for a wedding or reunion," Carol said. She notes that the business is primarily the gift shop and said that this is not a traditional B&B where guests share someone's home and receive a great deal of personal attention from the innkeepers. Plans call for putting a tea room on the main floor and moving the gift shop to an old one-room schoolhouse being moved to the property. During off hours, having the tea room there should give guests more use of the main floor than is possible with the gift shop, she said.

Rooms and Rates: Three - Only two rented at once. All upstairs, share bath with tub only; bath with shower available downstairs. Blue Room has double white iron bed, quilt, done in light blue and white. Peach Room has stained glass window, queen bed with an Amish quilt, done in peach and cream. Brass Room has double brass bed with an Amish quilt, sitting area, done in dark blue and white. $50 single or double. Add tax. No third person in room.

Meals: Continental breakfast is served in the kitchen from 8 to 9 a.m. and includes juice, rolls and coffee.

Dates open: Summer weekends

Smoking: "Prefer not"

Children: "Prefer not"

Pets: "Prefer not"

Other/Group Uses: No

Nearby: Restaurants, bakery, shops, antique shop, lake, 2 blocks. Biking around the lake. Boat rentals, 3 blocks. Swimming beach, 1 mile.

Driving Time/Directions from Twin Cities: Within 3 hours. I-94 northwest to Osakis exit. Go through town 2 blocks; inn is on left side of Main Street.

Deposit: Not necessary

Payment: Cash, personal or traveler's checks, VISA or MasterCard

The Country House

Rt. 3, Box 110
Miltona, MN 56354
218-943-2928

Owner/Operator:
Dianne Walker

Five hundred forty pounds of plaster. Sixty two gallons of paint. Sixty four hundred board feet of lumber. Dianne Walker counted it all as it went into a property in such sad shape that even the bank that owned it was thinking about tearing some of it down.

Walker bought the property in 1987 with a winter of work ahead of her. But she looked forward to it. "I needed something to do besides work for someone else's business," she said. "It looked like the kind of place that had had fun."

As a project manager for a restaurant chain, she had acquired "a lifestyle" in the Twin Cities. "But I turned 35 and I wondered, 'What am I going to do when I grow up?' " She took some time off after finishing a major project and visited her parents, who were vacationing at a nearby resort where they had spent many summers. She saw the old Evergreen Inn, facing Lake Miltona, was for sale.

The original Inn was built in the 1880s. It was first a stagecoach stop between Minneapolis and Fargo, then a speakeasy (local legend says that early notice of one raid allowed time to put the slot machines in boats out onto the lake, where they were dumped overboard). Then it was a resort until the 1980s, when cabins and much of the land was sold to pay off debts. The house stood empty for years and the roof leaked, so the plaster had rotted and the floor had buckled.

Walker had the roof and floor replaced. She plastered, put in new baths, redid the kitchen, stenciled the walls and floors and decorated. "This is not a fancy place," she says. Guests enjoy the fireplace on the summer porch, come in to supper in swim suits and help start the grill. The cookie jar is always full, and lemonade and other beverages are available.

Rooms and Rates: Five - Four upstairs share one full bath with tub and shower and one half bath. All with antiques, country furniture and quilts, pine floors. Legacy and Sunrise Rooms have double beds; Sunset and Lakeside Rooms have queen beds. Pine Room is on the first floor, has knotty pine paneling, double bed, private bath with tub and shower, private entrance. $45 Friday and Saturday nights, $40 other times. Rates are single or double. Add tax. Extra child over six in room, $5. Rates $5 less Oct. 1 to May 1.

Meals: Breakfast is served in the dining area at a time of guests' choice and it may include Eggs Mornay, wild rice waffles, sausage strata or apple pannekoeken, fresh fruit, muffins or rolls, cereals, juices, coffee, teas. Dinners available by prior arrangement.

Dates open: Year 'round   **Smoking:** By fireplace only

Children: Yes   **Pets:** Yes (dog on premises)

Other/Group Uses: Mystery weekends planned for groups

Nearby: Swimming, x-c skiing, snowmobiling. Walleye, northern and bass fishing. Golf, 1-12 miles. Restaurants, shops in Alexandria, 10 miles. Boat rentals at resorts next door; sailboats, sailboards, pontoon rentals nearby. Carlos State Park (hiking, x-c skiing), 2 miles. County park, 3 miles.

Driving Time/Directions from Twin Cities: Within 3 hours. I-94 west to Alexandria exit; Highway 29 through town 10 miles to County Road 5. Turn west 3/4 mile to corner, turn right. House is on lakeside between Tip Top Cove and Woodland resorts.

Deposit: $20

Payment: Cash, personal or traveler's checks only

The American House

410 E. Third St.
Morris, MN 56267
612-589-4054

Owners/Operators:
Karen and Kyle Berget

"I'd always driven by when I moved out here five years ago and thought, 'What a neat house.' It reminded me of Stillwater and I was homesick for it," said Karen Berget, a native of Stillwater, the St. Croix River town replete with turn-of-the-century mansions. She's stayed in the B&Bs there and spent her wedding night at the Lowell Inn, so it wasn't surprising when she and Kyle toured this Victorian home and thought it would make a good B&B.

Built in 1901, the house had 11 owners before the Bergets, one of whom was a wealthy judge and farmer who moved into town for the winter so his children could attend school. The home was cut up into a duplex in the 1940s, and remained that way until Bergets bought it in May 1984.

Starting, literally, from the ground up, they moved some walls, replastered, and did other major renovation. The restoration, which took six months, was not without its surprises, the best of which was in the dining room. Hidden under carpeting was a walnut and oak parquet floor known as a "picture frame" floor because of its design of walnut borders. The dining room also had original handstenciled wall borders, and Karen added her own in the guest rooms.

A study in the local historical society records provided the name for the B&B, taken from the first hotel in Morris, built in 1875. Guests can use the dining room, a toy room upstairs with TV and games, and "we have a bicycle built for two that we encourage guests to tour Morris on."

Rooms and Rates: Three - All double beds, furnished with antiques and quilts; all share bath with clawfoot tub and shower. Anna's Room, which used to be the kitchen in the upstairs apartment, has partial canopy bedroom set from old Curtis Hotel, Minneapolis - $35. Elizabeth's Room is in blue and white with handstenciled walls - $35. Christian John's Room has two matching antique beds, sleeps up to four - $40. Extra person in room, $2. Tax included. Rates are double. Midweek single rates.

Meals: Breakfast is served in the dining room at a time convenient for guests and includes juice, milk, non-alcoholic amaretto coffee, omelettes, buttermilk pancakes, sausage, or bacon, rolls or coffee cake, fresh fruit.

Dates open: Year 'round

Smoking: In designated areas

Children: Yes

Pets: No

Other/Group Uses: Small luncheons, business meetings, birthday parties.

Nearby: University of Minnesota-Morris, 2 blocks; bike path to city park, 4 blocks; city park with swimming, 1 mile; downtown shops, restaurants, 6 blocks.

Driving Time/Directions from Twin Cities: Within 3 hours. I-94 northwest to Sauk Centre exit, west on Highway 28 to Morris. Left on Columbia Ave. by the Pizza Hut, go up to the corner of Third and Columbia.

Deposit: Half of room rate

Payment: Cash, personal or traveler's checks only

Blanchford Inn

600 W. Redwood
Marshall, MN 56258
507-532-5071

Owners/Operators:
Kathy and Jerry Lozinski

Kathy and Jerry Lozinski say they owe their B&B to friends in Hudson, Wis. Kathy was a schoolmate of Sharon Miller, who runs the Jefferson-Day House, Hudson's first B&B, with her husband, Wally.

After a visit, Lozinskis were hooked. "I did day care for 18 years," Kathy explained. "We saw how much fun they were having doing a B&B and I knew immediately that this was my change of career." Kathy and Jerry, a buyer for a retail farm hardware and supply store, were born and raised in the area. They moved to Marshall when they married. They were eager to open Marshall's first B&B.

Lozinskis knew this 1908 Greek Revival home was for sale. Built by Guy Blanchard, the treasurer of Marshall's first flour mill, it's full of ornate woodwork that had been kept in remarkably good condition. A local doctor and his wife raised a family of four there until 1956. Then the people who ran a cement company in town bought it and raised nine children.

But such a big house, with three floors and a full basement, isn't for everyone. The home was for sale on and off again for about five years and was even vacant for a couple years before Lozinskis bought it. "Basically, we came in and cleaned and dusted and replaced carpet and built bathrooms and washed woodwork," Kathy said. Building the new bathrooms, though, involved 18-hour days for six weeks, staying up to 1 a.m. cleaning up to stay ahead of the carpenters.

The result is one of which they are proud. "We're just tickled to have this house to preserve and share with Marshall," Kathy said. They opened five rooms, four named for their children, in May 1988, decorated with antiques they restored.

Rooms and Rates: Five - All upstairs with window air conditioners. Tony's Room has double antique bed with birdseye maple trim, done in blue and white. Grandmother's Room has queen brass and marble bed, long lace drapes, done in rose, cream and green. Paul's Room has double sleigh bed and matching dresser of Russian olive, hand-crocheted bedspread. All three rooms have new private baths with showers only - $50. Marie's Room has tall double bed reached by footstool, shares large bath with tub and separate shower with Teri's Room, which has a double white iron bed, oriental rug, done in white with blue accents - $35. Add tax. Rates are single or double. Midweek corporate discounts.

Meals: Breakfast is served in the dining room at a time arranged the night before and it may include fresh fruit, coffeecake or a variety of muffins, sausage or ham quiche, toast and jam, juice, coffee and milk.

Dates open: Year 'round

Smoking: In designated areas

Children: If under 10, inquire

Pets: No

Other/Group Uses: No

Nearby: Downtown movie theater, shops, 3 blocks. Restaurants, 1 mile. Southwest State University and dinner theater, 2 miles. Camden State Park (hiking, swimming, x-c skiing), 6 miles. Walnut Grove (Laura Ingalls Wilder pageant), 35 miles. Pipestone National Monument, 40 miles.

Driving Time/Directions from Twin Cities: Within 3 hours. From Highway 23, take Highway 59 northwest to Sixth Street. Turn right. Two blocks to the corner of Redwood at Sixth.

Deposit: Half of room rate

Payment: Cash, personal or traveler's checks, VISA or MasterCard

Carrolton Country Inn

R.R. 2, Box 139
Lanesboro, MN 55949
507-467-2257

Owners/Operators:
Gloria and Charles Ruen

Ninety-one gallons of paint stripper, and almost as many pairs of gloves, were used by Gloria Ruen during this farm home's two-and-a-half year restoration.

"I'd just come over and shut the door and go to work" on the doorways, floors and cabinets, said the schoolteacher, who lived in the house with her family until they moved to a nearby farm closer to main roads. This farm is on the Ox Cart Road along the limestone bluffs and the Root River, crossed by the state bike trail.

Norwegian bachelor farmer Selmer Skarie last owned this farm, settled by his grandparents in about 1856. They lived in a three-story log cabin, the remains of which are through the pasture. Part of the farmhouse was built in 1882 and added onto about 1900. It was the first farm home in the area to have indoor plumbing. One local woman told Gloria about "coming here as a little girl with her mother for Ladies' Aid and all the little girls would use the bathroom all afternoon long."

Charles Ruen's father bought the farm in 1958. Then Ruens started to raise four boys on the 389 acres. When they moved to another farm, they rented out the farmhouse. But Gloria thought a quiet country haven for travelers would be a better use, and she set about restoration. New carpet, two new baths, storm windows and a septic tank also were added.

Today, Gloria checks in guests who have use of the entire house and tells them about it and the 45 cows, 45 calves and one horse in the pasture ("Don't leave the gate open or they get in the yard and eat the flowers"). Some guests have been lucky enough to see calves being born. Others see wild turkey.

Ruens also have a nearby farm cottage with outdoor plumbing, open April through November. Pets, kids and smoking are OK. It rents for $18 per person.

Rooms and Rates: Four - Century Room is downstairs with queen brass bed, private bath with clawfoot tub only - $55. Carrolton Room is former master bedroom, original picture rail and wood floor, queen bed, porch overlooking farm, new bath with tub and shower - $65. The Ageless Room is son's former bedroom, one double and one twin bed with red and blue spreads, shares bath with tub and shower with Betsy's Room - $50. Betsy's Room was Selmer's housekeeper's room, has double bed, done in blue and pink - $50. Add tax. Rates are double. Single, $10 less. Weekday rates are $5 less.

Meals: Gloria comes over to the house to fix breakfast at a time arranged the night before or breakfast fixings are left in the refrigerator. Breakfast includes an egg and sausage casserole, homemade mufffins, fruit, coffee, juice and milk, and a sign warns, "Do NOT do the dishes!"

Dates open: Year 'round

Smoking: No

Children: Yes

Pets: No

Other/Group Uses: Reunions, retreats and seasonal lodging for hunters.

Nearby: Root River State Trail (biking, hiking, x-c skiing), 8/10 mile. Canoe rental, restaurants, antiques, winery in Lanesboro, 3 miles.

Driving Time/Directions from Twin Cities: Within 3 hours. Highways 52 or 16 to Lanesboro. Take County Road 8 for two miles west of Lanesboro or County Road 8 for 7 miles east of Fountain to Gloria's farm (headquarters sign on lawn). She escorts guests to the inn.

Deposit: Half of amount due

Payment: Cash, personal or traveler's checks only

Lanesboro

Mrs. B's Historic Lanesboro Inn

101 Parkway Ave.
Lanesboro, MN 55949
507-467-2154

Owners/Operators:
Nancy and Jack Bratrud
and family

The Bratruds fell in love with Lanesboro and bought 100 acres in 1980. Jack and Nancy later bought an old building in downtown Lanesboro, pretty much on a whim. When the city wanted to keep that building for a museum and offered them "a much better building" across the street, they agreed. "We became more and more serious about leaving Minneapolis," Jack said.

Empty building in hand, they thought about a restaurant or office space. But the design that looked ideal was a country inn. The building, now on the National Register of Historic Places, was constructed in 1872 of local limestone from the cliffs in the Root River valley. "It had three owners," Nancy says, "the Thompson and Thompson brothers, the Thompson and Thompson brothers, and the Johnsons." The Thompsons weren't related, but all owners operated a combination furniture store/mortuary in the building.

Everything but the wood flooring was rebuilt, plumbing was installed for the first time, and the stone exterior was restored. "Our concept was to give guests a little more privacy," Nancy said, pointing to soundproofed walls. The lobby has a baby grand piano, and guests can use decks on side of the building. Guests receive complimentary sherry and chocolate kisses. Tea is served about 4 p.m. on Fridays and Saturdays. The restaurant in the ground level has a breakfast room, just for guests, and a dining room, sometimes open to the public for dinners. Menus feature regional foods, perhaps including Root River trout or bread with flour stone-ground at the Stockton mill.

Rooms and Rates: Nine - Eight with queen beds. All with private baths, seven have tub, two have shower only. Each room is different, but four have canopied, four-poster beds - $50 weekdays, $85 Friday or Saturday. Some have partial canopies. All others $40 weekdays, $75 weekends. Add tax. Extra person in room, $8. Other examples include #9, with a Norwegian "cupboard bed" requiring a small step-stool to reach; #3 is done in rose and grey, has two twin beds hand-carved by Jack.

112

Meals: Breakfast is included in room rate and may include wild blackberries, local sausage, fresh eggs, seven-grain pancakes and homemade breads. Dinners open to the public Thursdays, Fridays and Saturdays.

Dates open: Year 'round   **Smoking:** In designated areas

Children: "Not ideal but not prohibited." No toddlers   **Pets:** No

Other/Group Uses: Small groups and business meetings with meals midweek.

Nearby: Root River hiking, biking and x-c ski trail, 1/2 block. Museum, woodcarver's shop and winery, 1 block. Guided cave tours, fishing, hunting canoeing, golf and tennis.

Driving Time/Directions from Twin Cities: Within 3 hours. Highways 52/55 south to Rochester, then 52 south to Fountain. Left out of Fountain on Co. Rd. 8, eight miles to Lanesboro. Inn is located just over the river to the left.

Deposit: $30

Payment: Cash, personal or traveler's checks only

Scanlan House

708 Parkway Ave. S.
Lanesboro, MN 55949
507-467-2158

Owners/Operators:
Kirsten, Mary and Gene Mensing

This home was built in 1889 by Mikael Scanlan, one of the Scanlans who founded Lanesboro. His family was involved in several businesses, including the first bank, jewelery store and a lumberyard.

The Scanlan family owned it for more than 40 years, as did the second owners, the Borgan family. Mary and Gene Mensing are the fifth owners, having purchased the building as an operating inn in November 1987 and taking over the operation two weeks later.

Mary and Gene found the home during a visit from Galesville, Wis., where Mary owns a beauty and tanning salon and Gene runs a trucking service. "Mom's interested in a lot of things -- she's interested in antiques, for one thing," said 21-year-old Kirsten, who agreed to come back from Vail, Colo., where she was doing sales and catering work, to run the inn. Mary comes over from Wisconsin on weekends, and, at press time, they were intending to sell their home there to move to Lanesboro.

Kirsten reported a number of winter 1989 renovation plans for this National Register home. Plans include changing the heating system and replacing interior walls, re-siding the house and painting a four-tone exterior, putting in another bathroom and stripping painted woodwork. Before opening, they were able to re-wallpaper three rooms, repaint the innkeeper's living quarters and add a patio.

Oil paintings done by Kirsten and Mary are hung in several rooms. Guests will find some shag carpeting and modern furniture mixed in with Victorian antiques. The fireplace in the dining room works and is available. A large color TV, stereo, radio and board games also are available for guests' use.

Rooms and Rates: Five - All with window air conditioners and color TVs. Downstairs are two rooms sharing a bath with tub only, or rented singly with private bath at $90. One room has queen bed, other is former library, has double bed. Upstairs, three rooms share two baths with showers. The Doll Room has a double white iron bed, doll collection, done in greens. Jade Room has oil paintings by Kirsten and Mary, double bed, done in greens and pinks. Grandma Bell's room has double bed, done in yellows. $45 weekdays, $55 weekends, double. Single $5 less. Add tax.

Meals: Breakfast is served in the dining room or on the patio at 9 a.m. or a time arranged the night before. It may include Belgian waffles, egg dishes, quiche or omelettes, bacon and sausage, muffins, cinnamon toast, coffee and juice. "Champagne on special occasions." Picnic lunches available.

Dates open: Year 'round   **Smoking:** Not in guest rooms

Children: "Older ages preferred"   **Pets:** No

Other/Group Uses: Garden weddings, meetings, reunions.

Nearby: Ski and bike rentals at the B&B. Golf course, next door. Canoe rentals, restaurants, antiques, winery, Root River canoe and tube rental, Root River State Trail (biking, hiking, x-c skiing), 6 blocks. Fish hatchery, x-c trails, 6 miles.

Driving Time/Directions from Twin Cities: Within 3 hours. Highway 52/55 south to Rochester, then 52 south to Fountain. Left out of Fountain on Co. Rd. 8, eight miles to Lanesboro. Turn right, go to south end of the main street.

Deposit: Full amount or confirmation by credit card

Payment: Cash, personal or traveler's checks, VISA, MasterCard and AMEX

Touch of the Past

102 Third Ave. SE
Spring Grove, MN 55974
507-498-5146

Owners/Operators:
Helen and Paul Espe

Helen and Paul Espe had owned and operated a local supper club for 11 years when health problems led them to list it for sale. "He loves working with wood so we thought we'd get an old house" to fix up, said Helen.

But a number of factors led them to open a B&B. Helen had been reading about them for years, and thought their work in a "people business" could transfer to a B&B. The house, one of the nicest in town with seven kinds of wood, came up for sale. It was too big for two people to occupy alone.

The house was in fairly good shape, but it needed redecorating and some other work. The B&B opened in May 1988 and cosmetic work continued one room at a time. Floors were sanded, windows were rebuilt, the bathroom was redone, and new carpet and wallpaper installed. A contest was held in town to name Spring Grove's first B&B.

The woodwork includes burnt ash in the dining room, birch in one living room the guests use and mahogany in the living room the Espes use. Helen believes the home was built by the son of the founder of the Onsgard State Bank who had the first Ford dealership in town. The house also was owned by a local veterinarian, a local merchant and a couple who moved to the house as semi-retirement from a local farm.

The guests' living room has TV and a chess board.

Rooms and Rates: Three - All upstairs, all share large bath with tub and shower. Blue Room has queen bed with lace and ribbon comforter, done in blues and beige. Purple Room has antique oak double bed, handmade rug, wood floors, antique Jenny Lind youth bed, done in purple, white and yellow. Peach Room has double brass bed, handmade quilt, done in peach, green and white. $30 single, $35 double. Add tax. Each extra child in room, $5; extra adult, $15.

Meals: Breakfast is served from 7 to 9 a.m. in the dining room and it includes juice, coffee and milk, ham and cheese omelette and muffins or fresh fruit, French toast and sausage.

Dates open: Year 'round

Smoking: Not in guest rooms

Children: Yes

Pets: No

Other/Group Uses: Talk with innkeeper

Nearby: Snowmobile trails, a few blocks. Cafes, 3 blocks, restaurants, 6 miles. Hiking trails, start in town. Deer and turkey hunting, trout fishing. Winona, 35 miles. LaCrosse, 25 miles.

Driving Time/Directions from Twin Cities: Within 3 hours. Hwy. 61 south to Winona, then follow the map along Hwy. 43 to I-90 to Hwy. 76 to Hwy. 44. Located on west side of town on the highway.

Deposit: Not necessary

Payment: Cash, personal or traveler's checks only

Winona

Carriage House B&B

420 Main St.
Winona, MN 55987
507-452-8256

Owners/Operators:
Debi and Don Salyards

In 1870, Conrad Böhn, a sill and sash manufacturer, owned a whole block of Winona's Main Street. A church now stands on the corner where his factory was located. His gigantic home is near the other corner. The three-story carriage house alone housed six carriages and several horses, complete with stable boys' rooms and a hayloft.

Böhn lost the property for back taxes in the 1890s, but it survived several owners, including a dentist who added an office to the side of the house. Deb and Don Salyards bought it in 1977.

When Don, an economics professor and entrepreneur, took a sabbatical and the couple traveled, the idea came to convert the carriage house, which was not being fully used, to a B&B. The Salyards liked staying in B&Bs when they traveled, "and we both like people," said Deb, who is active in the Winona Historical Society.

Complete interior renovation included adding insulation, plumbing, wiring, soundproofed walls and bathrooms, as well as a four-season porch. The B&B opened in August 1986 with four second-floor rooms, two of which were the stable boys'. Guests use a private entrance, and have breakfast on the porch or delivered to their rooms. The hallway has a brass hitching post as part of the railing, and a refrigerator and coffee pot are available for guests' use.

Complimentary wine and soft drinks are included. Guests also may use regular bicycles or the two-seater.

Rooms and Rates: Two sharing a bath, plus two-bedroom suite which shares a bath. All double four-poster beds. Pedestal sinks in each room. Baths have shower only. Rooms done in "country" wallpaper and each has its own decor in mauve, blue, beige and off-white, with a resident teddy bear - $45 or $55. Two adjoining rooms rented together with bath - $95. Add tax. Singles $5 less. Extra person in room, $7. Anniversary packages.

Meals: Breakfast is delivered to the room or served on the porch at a time arranged the night before, and includes fresh fruit, muffins, croissant, sweet rolls, jams, juices and coffee.

Dates open: Year 'round   **Smoking:** No

Children: 12 and older   **Pets:** No

Other/Group Uses: Small business groups on porch, small city tour groups.

Nearby: Lake Winona and bike trails, 4 blocks. Mississippi River and levee park, 4 blocks. Armory Museum, 5 blocks. Community theater and Winona State University, 1 block. Antique and craft stores, restaurants, 3 blocks.

Driving Time/Directions from Twin Cities: Within 3 hours. Highway 61 south to Winona, left on Highway 43, which turns into Main Street.

Deposit: $25

Payment: Cash, personal or traveler's checks only

The Hotel

129 W. Third St.
Winona, MN 55987
507-452-5460

Owner/Manager: Macari M. Bishara

When it opened Oct. 1, 1982, the Schlitz Hotel was called "an ornament to the city" by the Winona Daily Republican. Costing $36,000, the three-story, Milwaukee cream brick hotel was "a piece of architectural work and substantiability for which this company is noted," the newspaper said, referring to the builders, Schlitz Brewing Co., of Milwaukee. A classy traveling man's hotel where women were not welcome, the paper reported a cigar salesroom and bar were on the ground floor with the dining room.

Somewhere within the next 55 or so years, the hotel did a flip-flop, turning into a virtual flophouse with $8 a night rooms. The Williams Hotel, as it was later known, was rumored to break occupancy records of sorts, renting one room 10 times in one night. It was purchased in 1980 and renovated. In April 1988, Macari Bishara bought it, with plans to upgrade service and add fine dining.

Restoration is most visible in the lobbies and stairways. The original backdrop from a local opera house hangs on the third floor landing. (The Chrysler advertisement on it was innovative at the time because it shows a woman driving.) The oak banisters are originals, and the original hotel desk can be seen now as second floor office. Also visible is an unusual interior brick wall. If ghosts interest you, check in to room #19, where a light appears early in the mornings and the door sometimes open mysteriously.

On the ground floor, Yesterday's serves liquor and food and has video games. Valet parking is available.

Rooms and Rates: 24 - All modernized with private baths (some with showers only), color TVs, phones and large window air conditioners. No original furnishings were left, so reproductions decorate the suites, such as the Princess Winona Suite, with a settee and marble top tables. Double rates $43 to $58.50, suites $74.50. Single $10 less. Add tax. Corporate rates, weekend packages.

Meals: Three meals available on ground-floor restaurant, Yesterday's, plus Sunday brunch. Lounge with original wood floor.

Dates open: Year 'round   **Smoking:** Yes

Children: Yes   **Pets:** No

Other/Group Uses: Groups 5-50 in River Room on ground floor.

Nearby: Winona County Historical Society Museum, 1 block. Riverfront park and riverboat excursions and dinner cruises, 3 blocks. Historic home tours, Polish Heritage Museum.

Driving Time/Directions from Twin Cities: Within 3 hours. Highway 61 south to Winona. Hotel located at the corner of Third and Johnson streets, downtown.

Deposit: Confirmation by credit card number

Payment: Cash, personal or traveler's checks, VISA, MasterCard or Discover

Triple L Farm

Rt. 1, Box 141   Owners/Operators:
Hendricks, MN 56136   Joan and Lanford Larson
507-275-3740

Minnesota's western-most B&B came about because "we both liked to travel but we couldn't doing farming," said Joan Larson, who traveled in B&Bs in Europe and worked in the Trapp Family Lodge in Stowe, Vermont. She and her husband, Lanny, opened their B&B in July 1986 on this 283-acre farm, about a half-mile from South Dakota.

"I feel our B&B is the kind I experienced when I was in Europe -- people open their home to travelers," Joan said. "We share a little bit of our life here." Larsons have 350 or 400 head of hogs on the farm at any one time, and guests are encouraged to see the animals and ask questions. Lanny will pick up piglets for close-up viewing. Guests also can watch the field work of raising grain, corn and beans, and perhaps take a lunch out to the men in the field.

Larsons bought this farm in 1977. Earlier, Joan and Lanny were teachers. But they also were farm kids at heart, and when Joan's dad needed extra help on his farm, they hired on. They bought into the hogs and then found this farm near his hometown while visiting his mother. They named it Triple L, "The Lord's, the lender's and the Larson's."

The farmhouse was built in 1890, and the present kitchen originally was the stable for cows and horses. "The farmers lived on the other side and kept the feed upstairs," Joan said. Over the years, the animals moved out, the house was improved and redecorated. A major addition was a large room with private bath in back, built for the mother of one owner. That area is what is used for guest accommodations, but their two children's bedrooms can be available for overflow.

Joan serves homemade ice cream upon arrival, before bed or for dessert for breakfast. Guests also can swing in the hammock, play with the cats and walk the country road to the South Dakota state line.

Rooms and Rates: Three - Downstairs, the guest area has a double white iron bed, queen hide-a-bed, rollaway and crib available, private bath with shower only. (Upstairs are two children's bedrooms which can be rented out, each with double bed. Upstairs bath is shared with the family and has tub and shower.) $35 single, $45 double, $50 family. Add tax.

122

Meals: Breakfast is served in the dining room at a time arranged the night before and includes fruit or juice, breakfast meat, coffee, and an entree, such as Belgian waffles, Danish egg toast, Swedish roll-ups or pannekoeken, or a farmer's breakfast of eggs, bacon, buttermilk pancakes and potatoes. A treat is served for dessert.

Dates open: Year 'round   **Smoking:** Outdoors only

Children: Yes (cots and crib available)   **Pets:** No

Other/Group Uses: Country breakfasts served six days a week for groups of up to 10 by reservation (usually not served when B&B guests are present).

Nearby: Country road biking and hiking, hunting. Fishing, swimming and x-c skiing at Lake Hendricks, 2.5 miles. Restaurants, tennis, pioneer museum, antiques, craft shop, auction company, golf in Hendricks, 4 miles.

Driving Time/Directions from Twin Cities: About 4 hours. Stay on Highway 19 west through intersection with Hwy. 271 for about 1 mile. Farm is on the northwest side of the road close to the South Dakota border. Map sent.

Deposit: $10 per room per night

Payment: Cash, personal or traveler's checks only

Lawndale Farm

Rt. 2, Box 50
Herman, MN 56248
612-677-2687

Owners/Operators:
Gay and Gordon Ekberg

Gordon Ekberg never went to high school, instead farming corn, soybeans and wheat and raising hogs on 400 acres settled by his great-grandparents.

Yet today, his office walls are decorated with awards and certificates of appreciation from wildlife groups all across the country. The only farming he does himself is of native prairie grasses, and the animals he raises are wild waterfowl.

To say Ekberg has an interest in waterfowl is a bit of an understatement. He's taken 103 acres, planted native switchgrass and constructed a system of ponds. The ponds have become home to 37 species of wild ducks, 14 species of wild geese, plus trumpeter and whistling swans. About 500 birds winter over here.

After years of reading scientific research and trial-and-error, he's been able to perpetuate the species. Some of the wildfowl progeny have ended up in the Bronx and Lincoln Park Zoos, in urban parks, and in suburban yards where residents have installed small duck ponds. Many have ended up appearing on duck stamps and in wildlife art, which Ekberg's sell in their gallery and frame shop. Also, he sells the switchgrass seed commercially.

In 1988, 5,000 people visited the farm for guided tours of the tall grasses and wetlands. The gallery, frame shop and snack bar were opened because of interest, he said. The same is true of the B&B. "People wanted to spend more time here, stay overnight," he said. The guest cottage was the pioneer farm home of Ekberg's great-grandparents. It was built a quarter-mile away on their farm and lived in by a family of nine. In 1940, it was moved to its present site. It's decorated with wildlife art from the gallery. The antique brass bed had a note that said it was purchased for $8.50, Ekberg said.

Ekbergs opened the B&B in 1987. Guests get a guided tour of the place and then are free to walk the trails and watch the wildlife.

Rooms and Rates: Separate guest cottage, rented to same party. Two double beds (one brass), bath with shower only, TV, small refrigerator, sitting area, window air conditioning. Some modern furniture. Deck overlooks wildlife ponds, has a picnic table. $45 single or double. Add tax. Extra person, $10.

Meals: Breakfast is served in the snack bar 7 to 9 a.m. and includes Belgian waffles with choice of toppings, sausage, juice, coffee, tea or milk.

Dates open: Year 'round   **Smoking:** Outside only

Children: Yes   **Pets:** No

Other/Group Uses: Group tours of the farm available.

Nearby: Walk 102 acres on mowed paths and old country roads, picnic on wooden deck or hillside near ponds, x-c ski on property. Bring binoculars. Restaurants in Herman, 5 miles, or steak house in Wheaton, 22 miles.

Driving Time/Directions from Twin Cities: Within 4 hours. I-94 northwest to Lawndale Road, five miles east of Herman. Turn north on Lawndale Road for about 1.3 miles.

Deposit: $10

Payment: Cash, personal or traveler's checks only

Hibbing

The Adams House

201 E. 23rd St.
Hibbing, MN 55746
218-263-9742

Owners/Operators:
Marlene and Merrill Widmark

In the early 1900s, only two doctors served Hibbing's booming population of miners and their families, many of them hard-working immigrants who came to start a new life on Minnesota's Iron Range. Both doctors operated an office and hospital from their homes, as was the custom before community hospitals existed.

The house/hospital of Dr. Bertram Sage Adams was one of the last buildings to be torn down in North Hibbing, the part of town which was demolished or moved so the Hull Rust Mine could extract the rich ore that ran underneath the city.

Adams' new home, built in 1927, was a striking English Tudor that was considered very modern for its day. Original blueprints have been found and the home cost $9,000 to build with its 12 inch-thick walls and $7,000 for accessories like a slate roof, brass lightplates and curtain rods, and leaded glass windows. Adams raised four daughters in the new home and built a large clinic next door. Several doctors worked together in the clinic and it is in business still.

The Adams family was "well-educated but not high-falutin'," said Marlene Widmark. For instance, the family had a maid, but the daughters had to pitch in on major cleaning chores. The family was well-respected and well-liked.

In 1984, Widmarks, who had been living in Hibbing for more than 20 years, bought the home from the Adams estate. "When we looked at the house, we realized a B&B might be a nice prospect," Marlene said. Merrill had taught in England for a year, during which time they traveled in B&Bs. But they rented the upstairs four-bedroom unit to college students while "the idea percolated for a couple years." After repainting and redecorating, they opened the B&B in summer 1987.

Guests use the former kitchen and living room as a lounge with cable TV and board games, and they can use the refrigerator and appliances.

Rooms and Rates: Four - All upstairs, decorated with antiques, and sharing bath with tub and shower. Two rooms have two twin beds. Two rooms have one double bed. All have matching floral curtains, spreads and dust ruffles made by Marlene, and are decorated with embroidered doilies, pillows and wallhangings. Plans are to add sinks in rooms. $30 single or double. Add tax.

126

Meals: Continental breakfast is served in the upstairs lounge at a time arranged the night before. It includes coffee, juice, croissants and muffins.

Dates open: Year 'round   **Smoking:** No

Children: Yes (crib, high chair available)   **Pets:** No (dog on premises)

Other/Group Uses: Downstairs living room available for groups/businesses.

Nearby: Downtown, 3 blocks. Historic high school tours, 5 blocks. Paulucci Planetarium and Hibbing Community College, less than 1 mile. Hull Rust open pit iron ore mine, 1.5 miles. Ironworld USA, 6 miles. Hill Annex mine tours in Calumet, 25 miles. Downhill and x-c skiing, biking, snowmobiling, state parks.

Driving Time/Directions from Twin Cities: About 4 hours. Highway 73 or 37 to US 169 north (to Chisholm). Turn left off 169 at the planetarium onto 23rd Street, go 8/10 mile to between Third and Second avenues. House is on right.

Deposit: $20

Payment: Cash, personal or traveler's checks only

Our Mom's B&B

323 Sheridan St.
Ely, MN 55731
218-365-6510

Owners/Operators:
Florence Forsman
Ron Forsman, son
Ruthann St. Martin, daughter

Boundary Waters canoeists who come out of the Boundary Waters Canoe Area and want a hot shower and a roof over their heads now have a B&B in an historic home in Ely. "Our Mom" is Florence Forsman who "talked my brother into buying this house when it went up for sale" in 1981, said daughter Ruthann St. Martin. Ron and his mother opened it in 1982 as a breakfast and lunch restaurant, serving downstairs in the home's dining room.

Florence had nearly grown up in this home, which was built in 1923-24 by Joe Mantel. Mantel's youngest daughter was Florence's best friend.

Mantel owned the hardware store then located across the street. He built the house for $15,000 and he and his wife raised six children in it. What he's perhaps best remembered for in Ely history is having one of the first cars in town.

Ron Forsman also owns a business across the street, the State movie theater. When he's not busy there or driving a charter tour bus, he's working at the restaurant/B&B. Either Ruthann or Florence is there every day, cooking and doing other necessities. Florence's grandkids are the wait staff.

Ron and Florence opened the B&B in May 1988, closing down the restaurant lunch business. "My mom had seen them around," Ruthann said of B&Bs, "and this way, Mom doesn't have to work as hard. She and I were working all the time" in the restaurant. Now they each work three or four days a week, she said, serving breakfast only to the public. Before opening, furniture stored in the attic was brought down, and no remodeling or structural changes were made.

A half bath is available downstairs, put into a former closet to serve restaurant patrons. The living area downstairs has a fireplace, padded rocking chairs and some modern furniture. Skiers can use the heated garage to wax x-c skis.

Rooms and Rates: Four - All upstairs, all share bath with tub and shower. All with some modern furniture. Two rooms have two twin beds. One room has a double bed, other has a queen waterbed. $30 single, $40 double. Tax included. Extra person in room, $5.

Meals: Breakfast is served in the dining room 5:30 a.m. to noon and includes a choice of eggs, bacon, sausage or ham, or French toast, or a ham and cheese omelette, and homemade hash browns and cinnamon rolls. Breakfast is open to the public "until the B&B is successful," then open to guests only.

Dates open: Year 'round   **Smoking:** Downstairs only

Children: Yes   **Pets:** Kennel in back of house

Other/Group Uses: No

Nearby: Located on the main street, downtown Ely. Shagawa Lake for fishing, swimming, 10 blocks. Closest lake access to BWCA (Fall Lake), 4 miles.

Driving Time/Directions from Twin Cities: About 5 hours. From Highway 1, come into downtown Ely. House is on the north (right) side of the street next to Zup's Supermarket. Neon sign on side indicates vacancy.

Deposit: First night's lodging

Payment: Cash, personal or traveler's checks only

The Naniboujou Lodge

H.C.1, Box 505

Grand Marais, MN 55604

218-387-2688

Owners/Operators:

Nancy and Tim Ramey

In 1928, a group of Duluth businessmen opened the Naniboujou Lodge, 15 miles north of Grand Marais. The mile of Lake Superior shore and 3,300 acres of prime land were designed for riding stables, tennis courts, fishing and hunting. Membership was by invitation "for those of standing," and included Babe Ruth and Jack Dempsey.

But the first members who came by bus or the steamship *America* found few developed trails and no tennis courts. After the stock market crashed, the lodge was foreclosed in 1932 and building materials for a third wing confiscated. The dream of a private men's club was gone.

Arthur Roberts then ran an exclusive resort, complete with valet service, but it closed after his death. Luther and Susie Wallace bought the lodge in 1961 and ran it for nearly 20 years, intending to turn it over to their two sons. But Luke and William, then in their 20s, tragically drowned in a 1977 canoeing accident.

Tim Ramey was their friend, and he and Nancy signed on as managers in 1980 when a Christian group bought it from the Wallaces. Rameys then purchased it in 1985. Tim and friends winterized and paneled one wing and new wiring and plumbing have been installed throughout. A solarium sitting room next to the dining room was added in 1983. "We don't have a liquor license and we don't have alpine slides," Tim said, "so it's more for people who want to get away from it all."

The dining room remains the Cree Indian Sistine of the north, with bright orange, red, green, blue and yellow art work. Naniboujou, the Cree god of the wilderness, is depicted on a wall. The stone fireplace at one end, with 200 tons of lake rocks in Cree designs, is said to be the largest in the state. The original paintings, hooped curtains and chandeliers remain. The building is on the National Register of Historic Places. In the rooms, the winterized wing has knotty pine paneling. The summer wing has Cree designs in subdued tones.

Rooms and Rates: 29 - Variety of queen, double and twin beds in rooms and connecting suites; private baths or communal bath with showers. Singles - $29 shared bath, $40 private bath. Doubles range from $35 shared bath to $60 for fireplace and private bath. Add tax. Winter weekend rate $110 per couple for two nights, meals included, $20 per couple extra for fireplace room.

Meals: Three meals a day available in dining room restaurant May through October. Winter meals included in group packages.

Dates open: May through October. Dec. 26 through February, open for weekends with two-night minimum, meals included.

Smoking: Yes   **Children:** Yes   **Pets:** Discouraged

Other/Group Uses: Weddings, groom's dinners, reunions, business meetings.

Nearby: Swimming in Brule River and Lake Superior beaches. Fishing, hunting, x-c and downhill skiing. Judge Magney State Park across the highway for hiking trails and to see Devil's Kettle in the Brule River.

Driving Time/Directions from Twin Cities: About 5.5 hours. Located 15 miles north of Grand Marais on Highway 61.

Deposit: First night's lodging

Payment: Cash, personal or traveler's checks, VISA, MasterCard, AMEX or Diners Club

Clearwater Lodge

CR 31, Gunflint Trail   Owner/Operator:
Grand Marais, MN 55604   Margy Nelson
218-388-2254
Toll-free 1-800-527-0554

Margy Nelson describes Clearwater Lodge "like you imagine old log lodges should be." The log walls are hung with bearskins, wolf pelts and snowshoes. A focal point is a huge fieldstone fireplace. The rustic furniture is hand-made from diamond willow. The porch looks out over seven-mile-long Clearwater Lake, whose name still means what it says.

This is exactly the type of place you'd expect to be run by a woman who loved living in Paris for 11 years, doing political theater. But buying Clearwater in 1986 meant coming home. Her parents had owned Clearwater since 1963, when she was 13. Her summers were spent helping run the housekeeping cabins and canoe outfitting business that was known as "Jocko's," after her late father, a Big 10 and Minnesota Vikings football coach.

Paris had "a lot of intellectual stimulation," Nelson said. "I miss that, but this place is pushing me as well." The summer-only business still is based on the six cabins and canoe outfitting, since the lake is mostly in the Boundary Waters Canoe Area. She added the B&B option in the lodge's upstairs rooms in 1987.

The lodge is the largest original whole log structure remaining in northeast Minnesota and it is listed on the National Register of Historic Places. It was completed in 1926 by Charlie and Petra Boostrom, area pioneers. Charlie, a trapper, built a lot of cabins in the area and he was the one who "hunted" the diamond willow and built the lodge's furniture.

B&B guests can take day hikes, rent a canoe or soak up the quiet on the porch or dock.

Rooms and Rates: Four - All upstairs. Two small rooms with half-log walls overlooking lake - $30 single, $45 double. They share half-bath; bath house with showers and sauna outside. Two suites, one with two double iron beds in one bedroom and one double bed in the other ($40 single, $65 double), the other with one double bed ($40 single, $55 double). Add tax. Suites have private baths with shower only. Extra person in room, $18.

Meals: Breakfast is the only meal served here, to guests only, in the dining room at a time arranged the night before and it includes juice, coffee and French toast with scrambled eggs and sausage, or an omelette with toast, bacon and fried potatoes. Trail lunches packed. Restaurants open on the Trail or in Grand Marais.

Dates open: May through October   **Smoking:** Yes

Children: "OK in suites"   **Pets:** No

Other/Group Uses: No

Nearby: Canoeing in Clearwater Lake. Day canoe/hiking trips to palisades or waterfalls. Border Route Hiking Trail to the Canadian border runs in back of the lodge. Honeymoon Bluff trail is 15-minute hike. Grand Marais, 32 miles.

Driving Time/Directions from Twin Cities: About 6 hours. Highway 61 up the North Shore from Duluth to Grand Marais. In Grand Marais, take the Gunflint Trail, follow signs. Lodge is about 30 miles up the trail.

Deposit: First night's lodging or confirmation by credit card

Payment: Cash, personal or traveler's checks, VISA or MasterCard

Young's Island B&B

Gunflint Trail 67-1
Grand Marais, MN 55604
218-388-4487
Toll-free 1-800-322-8327

Owners/Operators:
Barbara and Ted Young

Those unfortunates without relatives who own a log cabin on an island in a lake off the Gunflint Trail now have the next best thing: Barbara and Ted Young. (If your family squabbles, this is better than next best.)

Located on a sizeable island in Poplar Lake, about 32 miles up the Gunflint Trail from Grand Marais, the B&B is open year 'round. The log cabin was built in the early 1930s as a summer home for a member of a Minneapolis symphony who had meals catered by a nearby lodge and canoed in. The Young family acquired the property in 1952, and Ted and Barbara moved to the island in 1974.

Barbara or Ted meet B&B guests at the landing on the mainland, then take them across by boat (or ski over in winter). Joey, their 13-year-old, will give guests an island tour. The house is heated with wood and has electricity; guests use the Swedish composting toilet and sink, and the bathhouse has a shower for summer use and a sauna in the winter. B&B guests are treated to evening dessert.

Youngs have a beach for swimming and a canoe is available for guests' use. Moose and bear are frequently seen in the area and fishing and canoeing on Poplar Lake are popular.

In the winter, Ted runs sled dogs, and he and a partner will let would-be mushers have a go at the controls. They operate Boundary Country Trekking for Boundary Waters Canoe Area trips and participate in the Gunflint Trail's cross-country lodge-to-lodge ski-through, during which skiers stay with the Youngs at the B&B or in wood-heated Mongolian yurts as they ski along the Banadad Ski Trail. Youngs bring the skiers' gear into the yurt or B&B, then Youngs transport it to the next lodge or yurt while they ski the next day.

A summer yurt-to-yurt canoeing program has been added in recent years. Youngs plan to open a five-guestroom log B&B called "Poplar Creek House" in winter 1989-90.

Rooms and Rates: One - With a double bed. Extra sleeping quarters can be arranged. $45 single, $60 double. Add tax.

Meals: Breakfast is served in the dining room at 9 a.m. and it may include Ted's Baked Eggs (mushrooms, onions, bacon, cheese and nutmeg), homemade cranberry muffins, a seasonal fruit platter, coffee and juice. Other meals are available on the Gunflint Trail nearby.

Dates open: Year 'round   **Smoking:** Outside only

Children: Yes   **Pets:** No

Other/Group Uses: A summer B&B tour along the Gunflint Trail is offered with Pincushion Mountain, a contemporary home built as a B&B. Groups and families often opt for the Young's yurt-to-yurt skiing or canoeing programs.

Nearby: Swimming, fishing, canoeing and yurt-to-yurt x-c skiing literally out the front door. Hiking trails, hunting, camping, canoeing in the Boundary Waters Canoe Area, dog sled rides and mushing.

Driving Time/Directions from Twin Cities: About 6 hours. Turn left on the Gunflint Trail in Grand Marais. Young's landing is the first road to the left past the Windigo Lodge, about 32 miles up the trail.

Deposit: Half of room rate

Payment: Cash, personal or traveler's checks, VISA or MasterCard

Voyageurs National Park

The Kettle Falls Hotel

Voyageurs National Park
Ash River Trail
Orr, MN 55771
218-374-3511

Owner:
  National Park Service
Operator:
  Chuck Williams

Places don't get more off-the-beaten-path than this. To get to this historic hotel, Voyageurs National Park travelers pull in via speed boat or houseboat, on a NPS tour boat, by floatplane, or arrange to be picked up at a resort 17 miles away.

Listed on the National Register of Historic Places, the hotel re-opened in May 1988 after $750,000 worth of restoration, part of a $5 million package that also included electricity and septic systems, and will add new cabins and 200 boat stalls, said Chuck Williams.

Williams' grandfather bought the 1913 hotel in 1918 for $1,000 and four barrels of whiskey. The hotel originally was built to rent rooms to construction workers building a dam (to find it on a map of Voyageurs National Park, look at the northeastern part of the park). Two dams were built for the logging business.

Williams' grandfather, however, had other business interests. "My grandpa ran it as a cathouse and a drinking and gambling establishment." Prostitutes who lived in tents nearby worked at the hotel. One-armed bandits were installed in the bar. But the biggest business was bootlegging. "He used to get his sugar by the railcar-load," and it was barged in to the hotel. Stills were hidden in the woods. Chuck's parents met when his father went to rent horses from his mom's father to transport whiskey out over the ice.

While the rolling floor and tilted bar in the saloon have been preserved, times are much quieter now. Porch sitting is a favorite activity. Upon re-opening, service was slower than fast-paced visitors from the Cities may appreciate, and some amenities (like reading lamps in guest rooms) were not yet in place. Board games and volleyball are available free, and there's exploring and beachcombing, too.

Rooms and Rates: 12 - All upstairs, decorated with antiques and antique beds. All share three baths, two with tub and shower. Ten with two twin beds, one with a double and twin, one with double only. $43 per night per person in May, June and September; $60 with breakfast and supper included. Add tax. Fishing packages, lower children's rates, July and August discounts. Ten new rental units in two four-plexes and one duplex to open in 1990.

Meals: Breakfast available to guests only and it may include juice, pancakes and sausage. All meals served in dining room or on porch. One fixed menu for breakfast, lunch is ordered off the menu only, dinner may be arranged either way.

Dates open: Mid-May through Sept. 30   **Smoking:** Not in guest rooms

Children: Yes   **Pets:** No (dog on premises)

Other/Group Uses: Boat tour groups arranged through NPS; group discounts.

Nearby: Fishing guides, boats, gas, canoes, ice available. Transportation from Ash-Ka-Nom resort on Ash River Trail, 17 miles away, $25 per person, per trip.

Driving Time/Directions from Twin Cities: About 6 hours. From Highway 53 (to International Falls), exit Ash River Trail to Ash-Ka-Nam Resort. Contact Voyageurs National Park about special concessionaire tour boat trips to the hotel (P.O. Box 50, International Falls, MN 56649; 218-283-9821).

Deposit: $25 per person per day

Payment: Cash, personal or traveler's checks, VISA or MasterCard

Travel Notes

Travel Notes

Contents Grouped By Location

Contents Grouped By Category*

Please note that these categories were assigned by the author, who is fully aware that someone, somewhere is going to strongly disagree. Some of the decisions are arguable; please read the descriptions and the introduction, then decide for yourself.

B&Bs, continued

Country Inns:

Historic Hotels:

Farms actively worked by hosts:

Private Guest Houses:

Contemporary B&Bs

In an effort to make this book more complete, information on the following contemporary B&Bs has been included. Note that the author has not personally visited these establishments and has no personal knowledge of them.

Written information was obtained from each establishment and/or the Minnesota Office of Tourism. In many cases, no information was available about whether the facility has been licensed by the Minnesota Department of Health, whether credit cards are accepted, or other information that may be important to your stay. As consumers, you are encouraged to request that more information be sent to you and to ask questions about specifics that are important to you. Rates, of course, are subject to change.

These B&Bs are listed alphabetically by the name of the town in the address.

Woods of Interlachen Bed & Breakfast

7505 Interlachen Rd.　　　　　　Owners/Operators:
Brainerd, MN 56401　　　　　　Marilyn and Pat Kraemer
218-963-7880

Kraemers opened four guest rooms in their modern home near Brainerd's Gull Lake and Nisswa in May 1988. "Our emphasis is on a quiet couples retreat," Marilyn wrote. Guests are able to have shore access to the Gull Lake chain for boating and snowmobiling. X-c and downhill skiing nearby, and guests may use the fireplace. Full breakfast is provided on weekends, continental on weekdays. Four guest rooms, all with double beds, have Minnesota themes (e.g., Lady Slipper, Loon) and quilts and antiques. Two have private baths, two have shared baths. $30-$55 weekdays, $40-$65 weekends, double. Add tax.

The Inn on the Green

Rt. 1, Box 205
Caledonia, MN 55921
507-724-2818

Owners/Operators:
Shelley and Brad Jilek

The Inn opened in May 1988 after remodeling the 17-year-old southern colonial home. "We have enjoyed building our own homes and also enjoy traveling and entertaining," Shelley wrote. "We thought innkeeping would give us a chance to combine all three into a business." The Inn overlooks a country club on 10 acres in southeastern Minnesota's bluff country. A "pool room" has a whirlpool and sauna for guests' use. Full breakfast. Handmade and/or Amish furnishings, family heirlooms. Four guest rooms, each have a private bath. $27-$40 single, $45-$50 double. Add tax.

Walden Woods Bed & Breakfast

Rt.1, Box 193
Deerwood, MN 56444
612-692-4379

Owners/Operators:
Anne and Richard Manly

This log home is on a small, private lake in 40 acres of woods. Anne, a forensic scientist, and Richard, formerly a director with the Audubon Society, built the home themselves and opened their B&B in mid-1988. "Richard and I met in 1983 and decided when we married in 1986 to build an addition on his log home and make it a B&B, which we had each separately been considering for quite awhile," Anne wrote. Located in the Mille Lacs/Brainerd Lake region with year 'round recreation, the home is filled with antiques and items collected during their travels. Breakfast includes homemade breads and muffins and often wild rice omelettes. Four guest rooms share two baths, $40-$55 double. Add tax. Single $5 less.

Three Deer Haven

SR2 Box 5086   Owner/Operator:
Ely, MN 55731   Anna and Ross Randall
218-365-6464

Just a few miles from Ely, this log home overlooks Clear Lake, where guests may use one of the Randall's canoes for a quiet paddle or to drop in a fishing line. Breakfast is served in the living/dining room, which overlooks the lake and has a fireplace for use in the evening. For x-c skiiers, a sauna and a three-meal package are available. Anna and Ross "daydreamed for years about running a B&B," Anna wrote, and moved to the Ely area near the Boundary Waters Canoe Area to do so. Full breakfast. One room overlooks the lake and has a private bath - $65. Two rooms share bath - $50. Add tax. VISA and MasterCard.

Glenview B&B

RR 1, Glenview   Owners/Operators:
Garvin, MN 55132   Caryl Keith and Charles Reinert
507-629-4808

This prairie home is tucked into the hillside in the prairie of the Cottonwood River Valley. Wooded hiking trails and x-c skiing are on the property; lakes, horseback riding, snowmobiling nearby. Some equipment is available on the premises for x-c skiing, biking and swimming. Full breakfast. A pet is allowed in one room with private entrance, queen-sized feather bed, private bath, country decor - $31 single, $36 double, $39 with pet. Second room has king-sized waterbed and a private bath - $36 single, $41 double. Add tax.

Cedar Knoll Farm

Rt. 2, Box 147
Good Thunder, MN 56037
507-524-3813

Owners/Operators:
Mavis and Leon Christensen

Guests at this 138-acre working farm enjoy a big country breakfast in the morning and may join the family around the fireplace or TV for popcorn in the evenings. A large screened porch with a glass roof also is open to guests, many of whom come for a retreat from fast-paced city life, said Mavis. The new Cape Cod-style house is decorated with antiques and treasures gathered during the time the family lived in Germany and Pennsylvania. Located in the Minnesota River Valley, the farm has horses, Chinese crested ducks and Suffolk sheep to view, and guests may walk anywhere on the farm. Skiing and golf nearby. The three guest rooms have dormers and antiques. Three rooms share a bathroom. $35 single, $45 double. Add tax.

Lakeside Bed & Breakfast

113 W. Second St.
Graceville, MN 56240
612-748-7657

Owners/Operators:
Joyce and Chuck Walters

Two guest rooms are available in this contemporary home on Toqua Lake near Graceville. Joyce wrote that the B&B opened in September 1986 "to provide a needed service to the community and to make good use of our new house." Guests may use the dock for fishing or sunning, and also may use the deck and solar room. Golf, tennis and swimming beach nearby. Continental breakfast. Both rooms have private bath, phone and cable TV. $25 single, $30 double. Add tax.

Killmer's on the Water

P.O. Box 22
Grand Marais, MN 55604
612-748-7657

Owners/Operators:
Virginia and Marion Killmer

Located on Lake Superior, this B&B home allows beach fires with marshmallow roasts and rock collecting along the shore. The Killmers "have traveled in Britain three times and ·wish to duplicate the British manner of inexpensive private home bed-and-breakfast," Marion writes. They've been open for four years. Guests agree on a choice of entrees for breakfast at 8 a.m. or have continental breakfast later. Sherry made from local rose hips is served and guests are given a bottle of crabapple wine to take home. Two guest rooms share a bath; $25 single or double. A two-room apartment has private bath; $40 single or double. Add tax.

Pincushion Mountain Bed & Breakfast

P.O. Box 181-3
Grand Marais, MN 55604
218-387-1276
Toll-free 1-800-542-1226

Owners/Operators:
Mary and Scott Beattie

Beatties moved from Arizona to the source of the Gunflint Trail to start a year 'round business with emphasis on x-c skiing and hiking. Their B&B opened in 1986 and is three miles from Grand Marais on a forested ridge overlooking the North Shore of Lake Superior, 1000 feet below. Twenty-five kilometers of hiking and x-c ski trails are out-the-door and, in 1989, the B&B will be linked with the 90-mile Superior Hiking Trail. Summer B&B tours of the Gunflint Trail are conducted in conjunction with other B&Bs on the Trail. Country decor. Full breakfast. Four wood-paneled guest rooms, each has private sink; one with private bath. $52-$75 double. Add tax. VISA and MasterCard.

Bed & Breakfast Lodge

Rt. 3, Box 84A
Hinckley, MN 55037
612-384-6052

Owners/Operators:
Krissy and Will Fey

Feys described their lodge's decor as "rustic Spanish," and each room has a name a decor ("Lotus Blossom" room has oriental decor, bamboo curtains, Chinese fans, brocaded bedspread). Ten rooms share two baths with showers. Lounge has TV, couches. Full breakfast. $20-$35. Add tax.

Lindgren's Bed & Breakfast

P.O. Box 56
Lutsen, MN 55612
612-748-7657

Owners/Operators:
Shirley and Bob Lindgren

Guests at this Lake Superior home on the North Shore have four lakefront rooms from which to choose. They also have access to the shore for rock collecting and a sauna and fireplace (complete with moose head and snowshoes mounted above). Almost the entire interior is wood (paneled or log). The home is close to downhill and x-c skiing and hiking. Continental breakfast. Two rooms share a bath, two have private baths, one of those has double whirlpool. $70-$110 double. Add tax.

Crabtree's Kitchen B&B

19713 Quinnell Ave. N.   Owners/Operators:
Marine on the St. Croix, MN 55047   Beverly and Terry Bennett
612-433-2455

Guests stay in their own addition to the popular Crabtree's Kitchen restaurant, which features homecooked meals. The addition was constructed upstairs in the back of the 1854 building and it has four guest rooms plus a common area. William O'Brien State Park is next door with x-c ski trails, and the Stillwater-Taylors Falls bike trail runs right out in front. A deck overlooks the woods and guests have a private entrance. Breakfast is served in the restaurant. Shared baths. $40 single or double. Add tax.

Dickson Viking Huss Bed & Breakfast

202 E. Fourth St.   Owner/Operator:
Park Rapids, MN 56470   Helen K. Dickson
218-732-8089

Located near the headwaters of the Mississippi River in Itasca State Park, this home has a vaulted ceiling in the living room and a fireplace guests may use. Helen Dickson wrote that she started the B&B because "tourism is a major industry here, my attractive, contemporary home is paid for, I enjoy being hospitable and like the service business, and I enjoy people who are stimulating." Close to Heartland bike and x-c ski trail, Village of the Smoky Hills, Viking Epic Outdoor Theater. Continental breakfast. Three guest rooms, two share a bath. $19.50-$28.50 single, $25.50-$34.50 double, including tax. VISA and MasterCard.

The Farm Inn

RR 6, Box 114
Princeton, MN 55371
612-389-2679

Owners/Operators:
Millie and Wally Schimming

The Inn is situated on 320 acres originally homesteaded by the Schimming family in 1898 and now operated by the third and fourth generations. Schimmings opened the B&B in late 1987 but Millie has wanted to host visitors for years. The Rum River runs along the property and trails run by it. Garden crops include raspberries which are always served with the full breakfast. Guests may use the living room and fireplace, dining rooms, screened porch and patio. Antiques and family heirlooms are used throughout the Inn. Tours nearby of cheese making farm, saw mill, dairy and sheep farms or a wild game farm can be arranged. Lunch and dinners by prior arrangement. Three guest rooms share a bath. $40-$50 double. Add tax.

Bunt's Bed & Breakfast

Lake Kabetogama
Ray, MN 56669
218-875-3904

Owners/Operators:
Arly and Bob Buntrock

This 2600-square-foot home is on 20 acres about 1000 yards from Lake Kabetogama and the visitor center of Voyageurs National Park. The Bunt family opened it in 1988. They spend summers here and winters in Florida where they own a real estate firm. The B&B "is the first step in our plan to bring to Kabetogama overnight motel accommodations, meeting room facilities, a world class billiard and snooker emporium, a modern bar/grill/lounge, storage garages...and, finally, condominium units and an 18-hole golf course." Three rooms, two with private baths; sauna, hot tub, full kitchen, fireplace and billiard table. $48-60 single, $60-75 double. Add tax. VISA and MasterCard.

The Woodland Inn

Rt. 4, Box 68
Sleepy Eye, MN 56085
507-794-5981

Owners/Operators:
Jane and Lerry Peichel

This rambler is located along the Cottonwood River. Two decks, TV, fireplace, billiards and ping pong are available to guests. Full breakfast. Two guest rooms have a private entrance and shared bath. $18 single, $30 double. Add tax.

Tofte House

P.O. Box 2102
Tofte, MN 55615
218-663-7604
Toll-free 1-800-542-1226

Owners/Operators:
Donna and Eugene Utecht

This custom contemporary home has three prow fronts overlooking Lake Superior, 100 feet away. "My husband and I retired on the (North) Shore two years ago in a home built by our son," wrote Donna. "With eight children, four married and four grandchildren, we wanted lots of room for them to come home. However, when they aren't here, we found overselves with lots of lovely space to spare and so our B&B came to be." Lutsen ski area, 9 miles. A two-bedroom suite has a private entrance, bath and living area. Continental breakfast. $80 double, $125 for two couples. Add tax.

Traveling to Minnesota B&Bs?

A highway map, a copy of the "Minnesota Explorer" newspaper (published three times a year), regional publications and other information is available upon request from the Minnesota Office of Tourism. The Office also distributes a free B&B brochure which lists licensed B&Bs and inns in Minnesota.

© MOT

MINNESOTA OFFICE OF TOURISM
375 JACKSON ST., 250 SKYWAY LEVEL
ST. PAUL, MN 55101   USA
OUTSIDE MINNESOTA, 1-800-328-1461.
IN MINNESOTA, 1-800-652-9747.
IN TWIN CITIES, 296-5029.

Travel Notes

Ordering Information

• Additional copies of **Room at the Inn/Minnesota - Guide to Minnesota's Historic B&Bs, Hotels and Country Inns** are available by mail. Cost: $9.95 retail.

• Traveling to Wisconsin? **Room at the Inn/Wisconsin - Guide to Wisconsin's Historic B&Bs and Country Inns** makes a great gift for all travelers, with photos and information on 86 establishments. Cost: $9.95 retail.

• **Wake Up and Smell the Coffee** features 180 breakfast and brunch recipes from B&Bs in Wisconsin, Minnesota, Michigan, Illinois and Iowa - places small enough so you can literally wake up and smell breakfast cooking (other favorite snack, holiday and appetizer recipes, too). Cost: $12.95 retail.

TO ORDER BY PHONE using VISA or MasterCard, call Voyageur Press in Stillwater, Minn.: **1-800-888-9653** toll-free, or **612-430-2210**. Add $2.95 per book for postage, handling and tax.

TO ORDER BY MAIL, send a check to **Down to Earth Publications, 1426 Sheldon, St. Paul, MN 55108**. Add $2.00 per book for postage, handling and tax. Please make checks payable to Down to Earth Publications.

Mail to: Down to Earth Publications, 1426 Sheldon, St. Paul, MN 55108

Please send me _____ **Room at the Inn/Minnesota** at $11.95 each.

Please send me _____ **Room at the Inn/Wisconsin** at $11.95 each.

Please send me _____ **Wake Up and Smell the Coffee** at $14.95 each.

I have enclosed $_____ for _____ book(s). Send it/them to:

Name: _____

Street: _____ Apt. No. _____

City: _____ State: _____ Zip: _____

Travel Notes

Ordering Information

• Additional copies of **Room at the Inn/Minnesota - Guide to Minnesota's Historic B&Bs, Hotels and Country Inns** are available by mail. Cost: $9.95 retail.

• Traveling to Wisconsin? **Room at the Inn/Wisconsin - Guide to Wisconsin's Historic B&Bs and Country Inns** makes a great gift for all travelers, with photos and information on 86 establishments. Cost: $9.95 retail.

• **Wake Up and Smell the Coffee** features 180 breakfast and brunch recipes from B&Bs in Wisconsin, Minnesota, Michigan, Illinois and Iowa - places small enough so you can literally wake up and smell breakfast cooking (other favorite snack, holiday and appetizer recipes, too). Cost: $12.95 retail.

TO ORDER BY PHONE using VISA or MasterCard, call Voyageur Press in Stillwater, Minn.: **1-800-888-9653** toll-free, or **612-430-2210**. Add $2.95 per book for postage, handling and tax.

TO ORDER BY MAIL, send a check to **Down to Earth Publications, 1426 Sheldon, St. Paul, MN 55108**. Add $2.00 per book for postage, handling and tax. Please make checks payable to Down to Earth Publications.

Mail to: Down to Earth Publications, 1426 Sheldon, St. Paul, MN 55108

Please send me _____ **Room at the Inn/Minnesota** at $11.95 each.

Please send me _____ **Room at the Inn/Wisconsin** at $11.95 each.

Please send me _____ **Wake Up and Smell the Coffee** at $14.95 each.

I have enclosed $_____ for _____ book(s). Send it/them to:

Name: _____

Street: _____ Apt. No. _____

City: _____ State: _____ Zip: _____

Travel Notes

About the author

Laura Zahn is president of Down to Earth Publications, a St. Paul, Minnesota, writing, publishing and public relations firm specializing in travel. Her travelwriting has appeared in many newspapers and magazines.

Zahn wrote and published "Room at the Inn: Guide to Historic B&Bs, Hotels and Country Inns Close to the Twin Cities" in 1986. This book, "Room at the Inn/Minnesota," updates and replaces it. She also has written and published "Room at the Inn/Wisconsin" and is co-author and co-publisher of "Ride Guide to the Historic Alaska Railroad." In October 1988, she published "Wake Up and Smell the Coffee," a collection of breakfast, brunch and other favorite recipes from small B&Bs in Wisconsin, Minnesota, Michigan, Illinois and Iowa. In these Upper Midwest B&Bs, guests literally can wake up and smell breakfast cooking.

Zahn shares her St. Paul home with Jim Miller, her geologist husband, and Kirby Puckett Zahn Miller, who was proudly adopted from the Humane Society of Ramsey County on the day the Minnesota Twins won the American League pennant in 1987.